A Place of Promise

A Place of Promise

Lorie Garcia

George Giacomini

Geoffrey Goodfellow

The City of Santa Clara

1852-2002

Published by the City of Santa Clara

Santa Clara, California

Project Director: Diane Kay

Graphic Designer: Craig Thomas

Digital Specialist: Robert Pleasure

Photographer: Paul Becker

Editor: Tony DiMarco

Proof Reader: Arlette McDermott

This edition published by:
DK Solutions Unlimited

ISBN: 0-9724948-0-4
First U.S.A. Printing
Printed in China
98765432

First Edition

TABLE OF CONTENTS

1   FORWARD
"...A Plain With Good Oaks and a Good River..."

15   CHAPTER ONE (1840–1851)
"...A Country So Fertile and Scenery So Enchanting…"

33   MARY BENNETT
"A Mind of Her Own"

39   CHAPTER TWO (1852–1865)
"…Stores, Churches…Cottages in the Midst of Orchards"

59   CHAPTER THREE (1865–1900)
"All the Conveniences of a Modern Town…"

85   JOHN JOSEPH MONTGOMERY
"Father of Basic Flight"

89   CHAPTER FOUR (1900–1930)
"…Where Health and Plenty are the Portions of Her People"

111   CHAPTER FIVE (1930–1960)
"Threshold of a New Era"

129   CHAPTER SIX (1960–1980)
"Everything's Changed But the Tree…"

147   DONALD VON RAESFELD
"…Run with a Private Sector, Return-On-Investment Mentality"

151   CHAPTER SEVEN (1980–2002)
"HT2 — High Tech, Human Touch"

167   THE FUTURE
"...It's Going to Be an Exciting World..."

170   ENDNOTES

Grateful acknowledgement is given to the City of Santa Clara
City Council which approved the funding for
publication of this sesquicentennial book:

Judy Nadler, Mayor
Jamie L. Matthews, Vice Mayor
Rod Diridon, Jr., Council Member
Pat Kolstad, Council Member
Patricia M. Mahan, Council Member
John L. McLemore, Council Member
Aldyth Parle, Council Member
Jennifer Sparacino, City Manager
Judy E. Boccignone, City Clerk/City Auditor
Michael R. Downey, City Attorney

Special thanks to Bea Lichtenstein for her years of
research into the history of Santa Clara's past
residents and institutions, and for the generous use of her
collection of historic photographs.

ACKNOWLEDGEMENTS

This Sesquicentennial Commemorative Book reflects the contributions and inspiration of many people—people who deserve far more gratitude and praise than would fit between these pages. It was not an easy task choosing from all the old photos and other extant materials that had been gathering dust in Santa Clara attics for decades. But as the past was written down within these covers, adding the smallest of details to the great events of the past, we sought to create a livelier picture of history, one with all its color. So as you flip through the following pages, we're hoping you'll look with a wry smile upon earlier times, when rules and attitudes were different from today. And as you look at the faces staring back, somehow you'll know that you are intrinsically connected to these folks—modern and ancient, young and old—through the legacy of the City of Santa Clara.

To the Sesquicentennial Committee: Lorie Garcia, Geoffrey Goodfellow, Harvey D. Gross, Patricia M. Mahan, Jamie L. Matthews, George W. Wood III, we could never have begun without your vision, support and immeasurable assistance on this book.

We also wish to acknowledge the City Staff: Jennifer Sparacino, City Manager, for her wisdom and patience when the plan changed so many times. Carol McCarthy, Deputy City Manager, for the additional editing and praise along the way. Mary Hanel, Local History Librarian, for hours of organizing and gathering the hundreds of photos and permissions and especially for her amazing, tireless help. And Gloria Sciara, Committee Staff Liaison, for being available when we needed you.

For permission to reproduce their artwork and photographs, we are grateful to the following: Gerald P. Sullivan, S.J., Mark Hylkema, Lorie Garcia, the City of Santa Clara and the Irving Cabral Collection, the Sourisseau Academy at San Jose State University, the DeSaisset Museum at Santa Clara University, the Archives of Santa Clara University, the California History Center of DeAnza College, and History San Jose.

And the past could not be recorded accurately without Paul Conrado for information about his great-great-great-grandmother Mary Bennett. Mark Hylkema for his wealth of knowledge about the Ohlone. William A. Wulf, Los Gatos Historian, for his wonderful historic collection, Edward Peterman and the South Bay Historic Railroad Society for information on the Santa Clara Railroad Depot, The Sociedade do Espirito Santo of Santa Clara for sharing its articles of incorporation and the families who provided pictures of their ancestors, the early Santa Clarans who built the City.

And last, but not least, many thanks to the creative team for its technical skills and patience in pulling the work of three authors and many contributors into a beautiful, coherent publication—editor: Tony DiMarco, photographer: Paul Becker, proof-reader: Arlette McDermott, digital specialist: Robert Pleasure, designer: Craig Thomas, and project director: Diane Kay.

Michael Harney's reconstruction sketch depicts a typical Ohlone Village. Each village was formed by a group of approximately 50 to 100 people living in family houses, with the "chief" living in the largest cluster of houses. These houses were small hemi-spheri-cal dwellings constructed of bent willow branches covered with a thatch of tule reeds.

" ... A PLAIN WITH GOOD OAKS AND A GOOD RIVER ... "

Over thousands of years geologic forces shaped the area that was to become the city of Santa Clara into a place of great promise. Located at the southern end of San Francisco Bay, hundreds of feet of fertile soil were gradually deposited by numerous small streams that wound their way to the bay, which was fringed with sloughs and swamps. On the valley floor, open grasslands and groves of oaks created a vast mosaic carpet of level terrain in every direction, embroidered by wandering lines of sycamores and willows that marked the streams' courses. And the breezes, blowing in a southerly direction inland from the bay, cleansed the air that was said to possess magnifying clearness. This was, indeed, a paradise in the making.

Along with the abundant water and fertile soil, the Santa Clara Valley's climate of wet mild winters with only an occasional light frost and a summer dry season running from May to October, created an ecosystem rich in plant and animal life. This included a wide variety of nuts, berries, bulbs and seeds with shellfish, fish, deer, elk, bear, antelope, rabbits and seemingly endless flights of waterfowl.[1]

The first human inhabitants arrived in the Santa Clara Valley about 10,000 years ago. After their arrival, environmental changes along with the migration of different groups into and out of the area resulted in a series of cultural transitions, much like the Dark Ages and Renaissance periods of Europe. By 800 to 1100 A.D. the native inhabitants evolved into that group of people first contacted by the Spanish explorers, whom we call the Ohlone.[2] Many politically autonomous tribal communities were located within the boundaries of the Ohlone territory. Each tribal community was comprised of one or more villages, formed by a group of approximately 50 to 100 people who lived in several family houses which were small round dwellings built of wood, covered with a thatch of tule reeds.[3] The City of Santa Clara stands today on what was the northeastern edge of the Tamien tribal district. Three large villages, each numbering more than 120 inhabitants, were located within a four mile radius of this area; one at the mouth of the Guadalupe River, one on the lower Coyote River, and one about three miles to the southwest. Two tiny hamlets were located nearer, one within a few hundred yards of the first village and one about a mile upstream on the Guadalupe River.[4]

The Ohlone used bows, snares, and traps for hunting, fished in boats which they constructed from tule reeds. They gathered and stored the natural vegetation of the valley floor in baskets, with acorns from the abundant oak trees providing the staple food. While most of the resources needed to live were available locally, the Ohlone traded with other tribal groups in California, obtaining obsidian from the Napa Valley, shells from the coast and wood for their sinew-backed bows from the eastern tribes.[5]

OHLONE
HUNTER

Having bathed and rubbed his body with herbs, this Ohlone man sets out to hunt deer. Carrying a sinew-backed bow and disguised as the game he seeks by wearing a deerhead and antlers, the skin making a cape to cover his shoulders, he slowly approaches his quarry holding an arrow ready for his bow in his teeth. His quiver made of a whole fox skin holds main shafts and his pouch contains fore shafts and points. When an animal was struck by an arrow, the main shaft bounced back and could be retrieved and reused by attaching another fore shaft and point, saving the highly labor-intensive work involved in crafting a new arrow.

While searching for Monterey Bay in 1769, the expedition led by Spanish explorer Gaspar de Portolá became the first Europeans to sight San Francisco Bay when they crossed Sweeney Ridge, west of San Bruno, and beheld the sweep of the Bay towards San Jose. Ensign Miguel Costansó, the engineer with the expedition, recorded this event in his diary on November 4th, writing, "From the summit of this range we saw the magnificent estuary, which stretched toward the southeast." They spent the following week exploring as far as the Santa Clara Valley before returning, giving us the first descriptions of the valley's inhabitants and landscape.

Walter Francis Drawing, Bancroft Library

In 1769, the centuries old, relatively peaceful life of the Ohlone was interrupted and would be irrevocably changed by the arrival of the first Europeans, as Spanish explorers stumbled into the Santa Clara Valley in their search for Monterey Bay.[6]

Spain needed to colonize California to protect its interest against the encroachment of Britain and Russia, whom they saw as an ever increasing threat. Distance and lack of Spanish colonists had led to the development of the mission system, a system which played a key role in Spain's plan to keep California safe from foreigners. Under this approach, the indigenous people would be converted to Catholicism, trained in agriculture and "civilized" behavior. Then, after a period of years, the Spanish crown would return the land to these now Christianized Indians who would then be *gente de razon*,[7] Spanish citizens, who could colonize the interior of California.

On the first of November an expedition led by Gaspar de Portolá, traveling north from San Diego to Monterey for the purpose of establishing a mission and presidio there, overshot Monterey Bay, crested the Santa Cruz Mountains and sighted San Francisco Bay for the first time.

After exploring the area around the Bay for almost two weeks, where the Santa Clara Valley was described by a member of the expedition as "a plain some six leagues long… with good oaks and… a good river,[8] the expedition returned to San Diego. Portolá's second trip the following year was more successful—Monterey Bay was located. There, on June 3, 1770, Father Junipero Serra, O.F.M., founded Mission San Carlos de Borromeo. Within a year the construction of missions at San Francisco and a site at the southern end of San Francisco Bay had been authorized. Exploratory expeditions to select this site quickly followed. In 1770 and 1772, expeditions led by Don Pedro Fages explored the Santa Clara Valley noting the people and environment, and in 1775, Juan Bautista de Anza explored the area as far south as Hollister and Gilroy. His expedition crossed over a large river which he named *La Señora de Guadalupe.*[9] This area would become Santa Clara where Anza recommended a mission be constructed because of "the large number of villages, the availability of water, and the seemingly good pasturelands." [10]

Following Anza's recommendation, Father Tomás de la Peña, O.F.M., with Lieutenant Moraga and nine soldiers and their families, set out from Mission San Francisco de Asís on January 4th and 5th 1777, to establish a mission on the banks on the Guadalupe River. Arriving on January 7th, they constructed a temporary shelter on the riverbanks at a location the natives called So-co-is-u-ka, meaning laurelwood, where Father de la Peña celebrated mass for the first time on January 12th. Nine days later, he was joined by Father José Murguía,

O.F.M., bringing supplies, implements and the bells and cattle allocated for the Mission. This first site would be named *Mission Santa Clara de Thamien.*[11]

Near the end of January 1779, as a result of heavy rains, the Guadalupe River overflowed its banks, flooding the mission complex. After more flooding in February, with most of the wattle and daub structures destroyed, the mission site was relocated to a site further south on higher ground near what is today the intersection of Martin Avenue and De La Cruz Boulevard.[12] Here a temporary mission, again with palisade style structures, was constructed.

Between 1779 and 1781, Father Murguía was busy preparing a new permanent site for the Mission. The place selected for this third location is currently at the end of Franklin Street where it is truncated by the El Camino. "In 1780 the first structure of adobe bricks was built"[13] and on November 19, 1781 the cornerstone for the Mission church was laid. Construction of the church took two and one-half years, and on May 16, 1784 Father Serra dedicated *Mission Santa Clara de Asís.* This structure, designed by Father Murguía, was said to be the most imposing edifice in Alta California.[14]

Kuchel & Dresel Lithograph, Santa Clara, 1856

In April, 1907, members of the Santa Clara County Historical Society placed a cross near the confluence of Mission Creek and the Guadalupe River to commemorate the first Mission site. A plaque on the transept of the cross reads, "Monument Site First Santa Clara Mission January 12, 1777." This first site was named Mission Santa Clara de Thamien.

THIRD MISSION CHURCH

MISSION TANNERY

During the heyday of the hide and tallow industry, this structure was the Mission tannery. In the 1840s its operation was taken over by José Ramon Arguello, and eventually the site was occupied by the Eberhard tannery. It was powered by a large overshot water-wheel turned by the flow of water from the Mission zanja (canal).

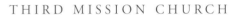

With the orientation of the church based on his archaeological discoveries, Mark Hylkema has created a drawing of the third Mission Church. This church, designed by Father José Murguía, was considered by several contemporary visitors to be the most imposing edifice in Alta California, and Father Junipero Serra wrote, "Nowhere else are the church and mission so beautiful." The view is to the northeast.

S.P. Saunders Photo, Sourisseau Academy, San Jose State University

Covering thousands of acres, the boundaries of Mission Santa Clara land ran from the Santa Cruz Mountains to the Guadalupe River, northeast towards Milpitas and northwest to Palo Alto. Part of this territory was used for agricultural fields to grow corn, peas, beans, and wheat and part as grazing land for horses and herds of cattle and sheep; the Mission's sheep ranch was located in Palo Alto near San Francisquito Creek. Besides the

selected territory, necessary resources were acquired from adjacent areas; wood necessary for construction came from the redwoods in the hills back of Palo Alto (today's Arastradero Road was the logging trail).[15]

Mission Santa Clara prospered, the harvests of its agricultural products were large and the number of converted Native Americans (neophytes) stood third in the 1790 list of mission statistics. Besides providing food for

In the early 1790s, construction started on adobe housing for married neophyte Indians at Mission Santa Clara. Eventually five rows, each containing six of these two-room buildings, were constructed, extending eastward from The Alameda to the front of the third Mission church. After secularization, four of these structures were part of an 1840 grant to Don José Peña, but by the early 1860s only the two northernmost rooms were still extant. This photo, taken in 1868 from the NE corner of Franklin Street and The Alameda, shows the Peña Adobe (the house at the left with the dormer and chimney) and another adobe neophyte house, the remaining structures in this row. Purchased by the Santa Clara's Woman's Club in 1913, today the Peña Adobe serves as their clubhouse.

the presidio at San Francisco, Santa Clara now also provided neophytes to help in its construction. In exchange, small squads of soldiers were sent from the presidio to serve at the Mission, the number varying from year to year depending on the availability of men and the need.

The increasing number of neophytes resulted in the expansion of the Mission complex as additional housing was needed, and many consider the housing con-

structed at Santa Clara superior to that at other sites. On his visit in 1792, the English explorer George Vancouver noted that under the direction of the Fathers a number of the neophyte Indians were "building for themselves a range of small, but comparatively speaking comfortable and convenient habitations—each consisting of two commodious rooms below with garrets over them."[16]

During the period of Spanish rule in California,

the Mission Santa Clara de Asís complex grew into an establishment with a sizeable number of structures, the church, the Father's apartments, storehouses, barracks, blacksmith, tannery, and laundry, etc. Construction of the Mission buildings continued through the first decade of the nineteenth century. From 1810 maintenance of existing structures was the primary activity with few new buildings erected.

A construction project unique to Mission Santa Clara occurred in 1799.

The location of the Pueblo of San José, established November 29, 1777 across the Guadalupe in close proximity to the Mission, had been highly controversial. However, the Mission church was the place of worship for the San Jose settlers. To facilitate travel for these settlers and perhaps encourage the worldly inhabitants of the pueblo to attend Sunday mass on a regular basis, Father Magín Catalá and the mission's neophyte Indians built the four-mile Alameda, a renowned avenue still linking San Jose with Santa Clara.

The road was raised in the center with irrigation ditches, which carried water from the Guadalupe River to the Mission, on either side. For the entire length of the road, down the center and along the sides, Catalá and his co-workers transplanted starts of native black willow trees from nearby groves. (These trees were mostly from the "Black Willow Swamp" later known as "Cook's Pond.")

The trees not only absorbed moisture, they also shaded the travelers from the sun and protected them from herds of cattle that roamed the pasturelands between the mission and pueblo. About 200 neophyte Indians watered and cared for the trees from 1799 to 1802.

After 1810, Spain no longer sent supply ships to the presidios in California, and by 1815 the missions had become their sole support. The facilities at Santa Clara were expanded for a great range of tasks, and by the time of change from Spanish to Mexican rule in 1822, the mission fathers acted not only as farmers, but also as bakers, manufacturers and traders.[17]

Concurrent with the change in rule, the Mission church and quadrangle of Santa Clara de Asís were relocated once again. A major earthquake which shook Santa Clara in 1812 and a second one in 1818 damaged the church enough to make it unsafe. A temporary church for use during construction was erected adjacent to the site chosen for the last complex (the fifth church and fourth compound).[18] Construction of this complex occurred from 1822 to 1825, under the oversight of the *mayordomo*,[19] Juan Ygnacio Alviso. First, housing for the Fathers was constructed and then barracks for the mission guard. Following these, housing for the young single neophytes was built and finally construction of the new Mission church utilizing material from the dismantled Murguía church was undertaken.[20]

After earthquakes in 1812 and 1818 damaged the third Mission Church it no longer could be used, so once again Mission Santa Clara was relocated. While construction of this final site (the fourth compound and fifth church) was occurring, a fourth church was built adjacent to the location chosen for the new compound. It was used from 1819 to 1825 when the new church was finished. Then, this small adobe structure served as a residence for neophyte boys and later as a dance hall.

This 1849 watercolor shows the fifth Mission church. The long building to the left of the church originally was part of the mission compound; however, by 1849 it was occupied by James Alexander Forbes and his family. The doorway to the right of the church leads to the Mission cemetery. This view is from the northeast.

By now vast herds of cattle ranged over the grazing lands (9000 head in 1831), and a very lucrative hide and tallow industry developed because, under Mexican rule, foreign ships had permission to visit the interior settlements along San Francisco Bay. Traders from the United States and England arrived and contracts were signed between the Mission and trading companies. Along with hide and tallow production, wheat and flour which was traded with the American fur trappers as well as the Russians at Fort Ross, increased in importance in the Valley's economy. While Mission Santa Clara benefited enormously from these economic developments, as there was little money available for the support of the mission after the separation of Mexico from Spain, the same factors helped escalate the end of the Mission's existence.

The increased trading in hides and tallow, led to a push for the division of the extensive Mission land holdings by the settlers at San José. Secularization[21] would benefit the pueblo residents in two ways: (1) give them land to establish large herds of cattle so they could compete in the trade, and (2) a ready source of cheap labor (the Mission's neophyte Indians) to work in the fields. The pueblo residents petitioned the Mexican government and in 1836 Mission Santa Clara was secularized. Its role became that of a parish church, and when the land reverted to public domain the Indian neophytes lost their claim to the lands which had been held in trust for them. By 1839, the Mission structures had started disintegrating and some of the neophyte structures were now occupied by Mexican citizens. The neophyte Indian population had started dwindling,[22] and September 1839 found those remaining "discontented and clamorous…complaining they received no rations or clothing…They demanded that no more ranchos be granted from Mission lands."[23]

The decade of the 1830s saw the beginning of a period during which Santa Clara would be impacted not only by secularization and the land grants made by the Mexican government[24] but also by the doctrine of Manifest Destiny, the American philosophy of coast-to-coast territorial expansion. The arrival of Jedediah Smith and his band of trappers in December of 1826 had signified the disintegration of the desert barrier against foreigners settling in California, and while restrictive Spanish laws prevented any real contact with foreigners, the new Mexican government was unable to deal with their presence. In dispatches Smith sent to the U.S. government authorities, he gave a picture of what was up to then a semi-mythical land, helping to set in motion a whole generation of settlers who crossed overland to settle in

Oregon and California. However, only a few of these settlers, who were mostly Americans and Englishmen, came overland with the intent of settling permanently. While eventually Mission Santa Clara was to be affected by American arrivals who "squatted" on the land and took up residence in the adobe structures, the earliest arrivals in California affiliated with the *Californio* population. They adopted to a great extent their host's customs and modes of living, and were content to follow a pastoral life.[25]

Historias – The Spanish Heritage of Santa Clara Valley, California History Center, DeAnza College

HORSE RACING

Trained from childhood to a life on horseback, the speed and endurance of their horses, their horsemanship and skill in the use of the lasso were qualities highly esteemed by the Californios. Popular sports which showcased their riding skills included grabbing a buried rooster by the neck while galloping full speed and horse racing. Horse racing was one of the sports frowned upon by the Americans, and it was banned by ordinance in 1852, shortly after incorporation of the Town of Santa Clara.

HAPPY TIMES

The gracious and hospitable Californios loved music, dancing and parties. Fandango was the term for an informal dance or other entertainment among the lower classes where friends and neighbors were invited in. Among the wealthy and aristocratic class, this form of entertainment was known as a baile, and was more formal and exclusive with invitations given more carefully. Both forms could include night after night of dancing, with seemingly no exhaustion on the part of the participants. While the everyday clothing for morning church services was the same for Californio women of all classes, a plain muslin petticoat and chemise with a long narrow cotton shawl or rebozo was worn on their heads or around their shoulders, at home and for festive occasions. The wealthier women wore more costly dresses made of silk or velvet, some with ruffled skirts and some trimmed with cherished imported lace, lace mantillas and richly embroidered shawls. The men dressed in cotton shirts and drawers with a short jacket often trimmed in scarlet, a sash about their waists and a serape or mantle, similar to but shorter than the ones used in Mexico at that time, botas (boots) of deer skin, secured by garters and around their heads tied a black silk handkerchief surmounted by an oval broad-brimmed hat. When riding on horseback their legs were encased in decorated leggings called gamuzas and the method by which these were wrapped was an art in itself.

As American expansionists began looking at California and reporting on what they considered to be Mexico's failure to improve a modern-day Eden, editors in the United States wrote that the local government was almost in a state of anarchy and that the local population remained content to do as little as possible to better their lives. As a result, newspaper readers came to believe that Americans could teach the *Californios* how to properly develop their lands. Adventuresome young men began moving westward and, because of Mexico's relaxed immigration laws, the number of foreign settlers began to rise.[26] The American expansion had begun.

WASHDAY

MODE OF WASHING CLOTHES IN CALIFORNIA.

Californio domestic life involved doing laundry and the "wash-day expedition" during the Mexican period was an event in itself. With the work usually done by Indian servants, laundry was done in a chosen place with plenty of available water, rocks to scrub the fabric on and an area with abundant sun in which to spread and dry the clothing. In towns like Monterey, laundry was done at the local well and was considered to be an occasion where the latest news could be gathered and passed on. On the ranchos, doing laundry involved an all day excursion which started before dawn. Great piles of soiled linen were fastened on the backs of horses with the women and children traveling in a carretta (a clumsy, spring-less cart pulled by a team of oxen) to the laundry site, either a spring or creek. There, according to Guadalupe Vallejo in her Ranch and Mission Days in Alta California, "the women put home-made soap on the clothes, dipped them in the spring, and rubbed them on the smooth rocks until they were white as snow. Then they were spread out to dry on the tops of low growing bushes."

" ...A COUNTRY SO FERTILE AND SCENERY SO ENCHANTING..."

The earliest foreign arrivals in Santa Clara were single men like James Alexander Forbes. A Scot by birth, Forbes came to California in 1831, became a naturalized citizen, and in 1834 married María Ana Galindo, daughter of Chrisóstómo Galindo, the Mayordomo of Mission Santa Clara. He came to achieve political and personal gain and apparently was quite successful in reaching his goals.[1]

Starting in the early 1840s, however, the type of immigrant changed when American families traveling in small groups overland via Oregon began to appear in California. They came to an area described as "a country so fertile and scenary so enchanting",[2] "for farm land, pasture lands, for peaceful home life."[3] These families arrived at a time when the mission system was in disarray and the political system in upheaval. The concept of California's independence from Mexico had emerged.

In April, 1840, 120 foreigners were arrested in California, including Isaac Graham [4] and 46 of his followers, and charged with conspiracy to overthrow the government. Then, in September 1842, Mexican and California authorities were alerted to the intentions of the Americans when Thomas Catesby Jones, Commander of the United States Navy Pacific Squadron, sailed into Monterey and seized the province, having heard a false rumor of war. The same year, the Hastings-Lovejoy party reached Oregon and the next spring part of the party came on to California.[5] These immigrants included two people who figured

Illustration by Andrew P. Hill, 1914, History San Jose

Captⁿ Weber
Mounted rangers

Captⁿ Marsden – U.S. Marines

Sailing Master De Young U
artillery

Naval Sketches of he War on C

Capitano Sanche comm^g as California

prominently in early Santa Clara history — George Bellomy and Mary Bennett.

By July 1844, when word was received that Texas had signed an annexation treaty with the United States and it became obvious that Mexico and the United States would soon be at war,[6] there were only a few American families living near Mission Santa Clara. The "Great Migration" of 1846 completely altered this.

That year an estimated 2,700 immigrants, consisting of entire families, headed for California and Oregon. Upon their arrival at Sutter's Fort in California, these 1846 immigrants were informed by Col. John C.

Painting by William H. Meyers, FDR Library, Hyde Park, NY

THE BATTLE OF SANTA CLARA

The Battle of Santa Clara, January 2-7, 1847, was the only campaign fought in the Northern district of California between Californios and United States forces during the Mexican-American war. In the 1840s an oak forest grew near the present Lawrence Expressway, but brackish water and marshy soil limited tree growth in the region to the east, providing an unobstructed view of Mission Santa Clara three miles ahead. The "battle" took place on this open plain. As the American Expeditionary force emerged from the trees, on a road that reached the present El Camino Real at Pomeroy Avenue, they first sighted the deployed rancheros. When the American's cannon became mired in the mud, halting their march, the rancheros came closer. An exchange of gunfire occurred with no one being hurt, and the rancheros returned to their camp within sight of the people watching from the Mission rooftops. After extracting their cannon from the mud the Americans continued to the Mission. The skirmishing lasted approximately two hours, but it took five days of negotiations before the official treaty ceremony ended the Battle of Santa Clara.

Fremont and the newspaper *Californian* that they could shelter during the rainy season at a number of "mostly unoccupied" missions.[7] Among the Missions targeted for settlement was Mission Santa Clara de Asís. In little over one month, from mid-October through November, 175 adults and children arrived at the Mission.[8]

In disrepair because of years of neglect, all of the mission quarters were inadequate by American standards. The immigrants lived in what they would later describe as "deplorable conditions, sharing a large warehouse building with little light. It was raining and the roof leaked. Food was in short supply."[9] With few of the immigrants understanding Spanish or the customs and manners of the *Californios*, many sincere offers of hospitality were refused.[10]

The American settlers began to feel far from safe, and believed that, should the need for defense arise, no time should be lost in preparing for an emergency. The lack of understanding between the two cultures culminated with the Battle of Santa Clara on January 2, 1847, the only campaign in the Northern District of California between the *Californios* and United States forces during the Mexican-American war.[11]

By spring, 1847, the immigrants occupying the adobe buildings at the Mission compound had set up a school[12] and were holding Protestant church services. *"Some paid rent to…Father Real…others simply "squatted"* *refusing to vacate the premises."*[13] In the area surrounding the Mission compound a small town of squatters' canvas tents had developed,[14] and in October 1847, Father Suárez del Real hired William Campbell to make a survey of the Mission land and draw up a town plan. Father Real then sold parcels following General Castro's 1846 authorization to do so.[15]

Except for the rise in American immigration, the months immediately following the Battle of Santa Clara brought little outward change. Then, on January 24, 1848, nine days prior to the signing of the Treaty of Guadalupe Hidalgo, which ended the Mexican-American War, James Marshall found gold at Coloma. Not many days passed before the news of the discovery was *"circu-*

THE FIRST SURVEY

In October 1847, Father Suárez del Real hired William Campbell to survey lots near the Mission complex, on Mission land, and draw up a town plat — the beginning of the Town of Santa Clara. These lots were to be 300 feet square, and were allocated one lot per person on which a home was to be built. Three months were given to accomplish the improvements and if they were not done, the lot would go to someone else. While it has been said that this survey and its lots were later declared invalid, the recordation of the first official town survey in August 1866 states differently with witnesses attesting that, "this [1866] map correctly represents the blocks, streets and squares of the said town as surveyed in the year 1847; and…that the land…has been occupied and used for town purposes ever since."

Alice Hare Photo, Santa Clara Woman's Club Archives

The Mission pear orchard played an important role in Santa Clara's early history both during the Gold Rush, when fresh fruit was at a premium, and in the initial years of agricultural development when cuttings from it provided the start of early orchards. Because of its economic importance, title to this 15 acre orchard became highly controversial and hotly contested.

lated with electrical rapidity through the territory."[16]

The discovery of gold and the subsequent rush to the gold fields resulted in an exodus to the mining areas of anyone in California who could leave home. The Santa Clara Valley was no exception; it was nearly depopulated. Even Father Suárez del Real joined the many gold seekers from the area.[17] By the end of 1848, some residents returned and found that the price of provisions had soared dramatically because of the unharvested crops.[18] Fresh produce both for those living in the Santa Clara area and for sale to the miners became very valuable. Because it produced quantities of the golden fruit, Santa Clara's mission pear orchard gained major economic importance. It quickly became apparent that there was more "gold" to be gathered in agriculture than in mining pursuits, and increasing numbers of newcomers settled on the land to make their fortunes, in large part paying little heed to the actual ownership of the land. They saw it as vacant and unused.[19]

With the influx of people greater than the outflow, the area around Santa Clara looked like a half military and half civilian settlement, with numerous white tents dotting the plain. The need for housing, both rooms and homes, became a major concern with the flood of immigrants. In addition to his tannery yard

business, George Bellomy established the first hotel in Santa Clara in 1849, the Bellomy or Santa Clara House.[20] In 1850, the Union Hotel, was erected at the southeast corner of Franklin and Main Streets. Prior to the arrival of the American immigrants, the vast majority of construction was adobe but the Americans did not consider adobe structures as suitable for permanent housing.[21] Producing the needed lumber for frame houses and brick making quickly became profitable enterprises (sawmills had early on been established in the Coast Ranges) and the growing demand for frame housing far exceeded the supply. As a result, entrepreneurs imported pre-fabricated houses from New England by ship around the Horn. The material for the houses arrived ready to be put together using only an axe and hammer. Commodore Stockton imported several to place on the land he owned (*El Potrero de Santa Clara* or the Stockton Rancho), and in 1850 Peleg Rush imported twenty-three houses from Boston and set them up in town.[22]

Along with construction-related enterprises, agricultural development along American lines quickly began. Impressed by the productivity of the Mission's orchards,[23] some farmers started planting small orchards and vineyards, some experimenting with these on the land they had intended for wheat farms.[24] After the Mexican–American

War was over Joseph Aram had stayed in Santa Clara and established an orchard nursery instead of joining those going to the mines. From 350 trees, mostly apples purchased from Aram's nursery at $1.25 per tree, E.W. Case planted the first American orchards in Santa Clara in 1850, located on property fronting Alviso Road.

"In 1850 California (and Santa Clara) was in the midst of social, environmental, and economic change unparalleled in world history—before or since."[25] On September 9, California was admitted as the thirty-first state in the Union[26] and Santa Clara County became one of the first twenty-seven counties in the new state with a population between 4,000 and 6,764 people.[27] The first college in California was soon to be established in Santa Clara when the Franciscan Mission itself was converted into a Jesuit college.

In December 1850, when Reverend Joseph Alemany arrived as bishop of the diocese, only one priest, Father Suárez del Real, was in charge of the Mission. The Mission's adobe buildings were in sad condition with most of the land being occupied by squatters.[28] As a means to save the remnants of the Mission and to meet the growing need for an educational institution, in February, 1851 Bishop Alemany invited the Jesuit Fathers to come to Santa Clara, offering the Mission to them for the purpose of opening a school, and the invitation was accepted. With the transfer taking place officially on March 19, 1851,[29] Father Real left California, returning to Mexico, and in May, Father John Nobili, as president, opened the doors of the new college to a dozen students.[30]

Meanwhile in the young town, besides the economic opportunities provided by agricultural endeavors, the newly arrived immigrants also saw opportunities for businesses that provided the goods and services necessary for daily life. Antonio Fatjo arrived in 1848 and, together with José Arques who arrived in 1849 (both immigrants from Spain), established the Farmer's Store. Dr. Henry H. Warburton (originally from England) also arrived in 1848, moved to a residence near Santa Clara Mission, became Santa Clara's first practicing physician[31] and established the first drug store.[32] The Homer Knowles Pottery Company, which like the tannery would become an important manufacturing company in Santa Clara, started manufacturing fine earthenware pottery in 1849.[33] In 1851, S.S. Johnson and Charles Clayton established a steam flour mill in Santa Clara, reputed to be the first steam flour mill in California, on the corner of Bellomy Street and The Alameda. Drawing water from Cook's Pond, the original structure in all likelihood had been the Mission gristmill as it was often referred to as the "Old Adobe" gristmill.[34]

In 1850, the first actual schoolhouse, long known as the "Little Brick School," was built by subscription on Liberty (now Homestead) Street.[35] (This location is where Saint Clare's Church stands today).[36] In addition to the establishment of Santa Clara College by the Jesuits, the Methodists also addressed the need for higher education. They established a college for boys on land near what is today the corner of Winchester Boulevard and Bellomy Street. Originally chartered as the California Wesleyan College on July 10, 1851, the following year the name was changed to University of the Pacific.[37] (It would be relocated to San Jose in the 1870s and in the 1920s to Stockton).

By 1852, a small hamlet of some 200 people living in a cluster of adobes and simple frame houses had grown up around the Mission.[38] Here, the enterprising American immigrants, within four and one-half years after the signing of the Treaty of Guadalupe Hidalgo, would formally establish the Town of Santa Clara.

A CANNY SCOT

At the age of 26, James Alexander Forbes arrived in California and quickly became a naturalized Mexican citizen, three years later marrying the daughter of Mission Santa Clara's mayordomo. By 1836 he was serving as the Hudson Bay Company's agent in Alta California, and in 1841 moved to Monterey where he became the British vice-consul. A man of many interests, Forbes was granted Rancho El Potrero de Santa Clara in 1844. In 1846 he was involved with Father Suárez del Real in the initial development of what would become the New Almaden quicksilver mine and the following year he played a role in the Battle of Santa Clara. When Father Nobili arrived in 1851 to establish the College of Santa Clara he found Forbes and his family living in part of the Mission quadrangle. Following a complicated negotiation, Forbes agreed to move and constructed the first brick house in Santa Clara, a building later purchased by the Sisters of Notre Dame to house the Academy of Notre Dame. Later Forbes built and operated the "Santa Rosa Brand" flour mill in Los Gatos, losing much of his fortune in this venture.

CROSSING THE PLAINS

Following the arrival of the Murphy-Stephens party in 1844, which opened the California Trail, thousands of American immigrants trekked across the plains and mountains to California. At first led by promises of land and later lured by gold, they continued to make this arduous journey into the 1850s.

THE CALIFORNIA HOTEL

Photographed in 1856, the large two-story building to the right of the Mission church was called the "California Hotel." Prior to the addition of the second story, this was a one-story structure that served as the Mission granary. It was here that the immigrants who arrived in the fall of 1846 spent the winter. Following the building's collapse in the 1906 earthquake, Santa Clara University's O'Connor Hall was erected on this site.

Photo of Unknown Provenance, Lorie Garcia Historical Collection

Because of the demand for lumber to build the type of houses the American immigrants
wanted — wood rather than adobe — logging quickly became a profitable venture. Just a
few years after the arrival of the first large group of immigrant families in 1846, sawmills
were being constructed in the redwood forests of the Santa Cruz Mountains. William
Campbell's mill, on what is today Saratoga Creek near present-day Saratoga, was one of
the first, in operation by the fall of 1848.

With the need for frame houses quickly out-pacing the available resources necessary to build them, pre-fabricated homes were shipped from New England around the Horn to Santa Clara. In 1851, Samuel Johnson, a Santa Clara businessman and civic leader, erected one of the 23 homes that Peleg Rush had imported from Boston the previous year. Located at 1159 Main Street, it still stands today.

FATHER
MICHAEL
ACCOLTI

California was not a field of Jesuit missionary activity before 1849. The co-founder of the College of Santa Clara in 1851, Father Accolti, an Italian Jesuit, was also the driving force behind the Jesuits coming to California from Oregon for religious and educational work.

Thompson & West's Historical Atlas Illustration of Santa Clara County, 1876

*Located at the corner of Franklin and Main
Street in the Arques Block, this general store
was established in 1849, by Antonio Fatjo and
José Arques, both originally from Spain. Later,
known as John Fatjo and Son, the store would
continue to provide staples to the residents of
Santa Clara, in particular to the newly arrived
immigrants from Spain and Portugal.
Members of the Fatjo family operated the store
into the first decades of the twentieth century.*

DR. HENRY HULME WARBURTON

Dr. Henry Hulme Warburton (1819-1903) arrived in Santa Clara in 1848 and became the town's first physician. Besides ministering to the local residents, his calls could easily require a day's journey in each direction as, at the time of his arrival, there were only three doctors in all of California. This resulted in a practice for Dr. Warburton that covered many miles of territory. In spite of the demands of his profession, the doctor found time to contribute both politically and civically to the development of the young Town of Santa Clara. He served on the Town Board of Trustees in 1854 and as an active member of the Methodist church and Odd Fellows Lodge No. 52.

THE WARBURTON PHARMACY

Besides initiating the first medical practice in Santa Clara, in 1851, Dr. Henry H. Warburton established Santa Clara's first pharmacy. Located on Main Street, the pharmacy is shown in this photo taken just three days before the building was destroyed on November 4, 1906, by a rapidly spreading fire which had broken out in Josiah Rainey's Livery Stable.

FIRST DO NO HARM

Originally located on the corner of Main and Benton Streets, Dr. Warburton's office was later used by Dr. George W. Fowler and then by Dr. Gallup, a dentist. Moved during the redevelopment of Santa Clara's downtown, today this office is located on the grounds of the San Jose Historical Museum.

RESIDENCE OF DR. HENRY H. WARBURTON

In 1886, Dr. Warburton constructed his home at 714-715 Main Street, directly across the street from that of Luis Antonio Arguello. After its construction, he used the lower floor for an office and pharmacy.

Mary (Anthony) Pascoe, Bea Lichtenstein Collection

Born in Plattsburg, New York, Dr. Arthur Wellsley Saxe (1820-1891) came across the plains to California in 1850. After practicing medicine in various sections of the gold mining region of the Sierra foothills, he moved to Santa Clara in 1851, where he practiced for many years, gaining a statewide reputation as a skillful physician and surgeon. In 1880, when he was 60, Dr. Saxe became president of the California State Medical Society and entered the political arena. He represented his district in the California State Senate in 1884.

Pictured with his grand-daughter Helen and son Frank, Dr. Saxe is shown standing on the porch of the office he built on Main Street adjoining his home. Later this office was moved around the corner to its present location, next to Dr. Paul's home at Benton and Washington Streets.

Mary (Anthony) Pascoe, Bea Lichtenstein Collection

In 1852, the year after his arrival, Dr. Saxe's wife, Mary and their two children Frederick, age 6, and Libby, age 4, joined him in Santa Clara. They traveled by sea and across the Isthmus of Panama because he did not want them to have to endure the arduous overland trip.

Mary (Anthony) Pascoe, Bea Lichtenstein Collection

THE SAXE FAMILY

An avid horticulturist, Dr. Saxe, after constructing a Greek Revival style home, which still exists at the corner of Main and Benton Streets, had extensive floral and botanical gardens planted on the property. Pictured visiting with friends in these gardens are Mary (Judson) Saxe (the gray-haired lady at center back), granddaughter Mabel, son Dr. Francis Keith Saxe and his wife Mary Jane (Cook) Saxe and Dr. A.W. Saxe seated in front.

JAMES MONROE KENYON

The Valley's rich soil and the immediate need for flour to feed the miners resulted in wheat becoming the dominant crop raised by farmers in the area surrounding Santa Clara, a situation which would continue during the first three decades of the town's existence. In 1849, following a six-month wagon trip, James Monroe Kenyon, his wife Martha and daughter Sarah arrived in California where, like others, he first searched for gold and then turned to farming. In 1850 he purchased 242 acres two miles west of Santa Clara on the Homestead Road where he cultivated hay and grain. Later, about 13 acres were devoted to prunes.

THE KENYON HOME AND WINDMILL

In 1851, the Kenyons built a home on their farm and for almost 100 years the family inhabited it. Five children were born and raised here and James and Martha lived in this home for 56 years, until they died in 1907 within a few days of each other. The farm was then divided among the children with Frank receiving the homestead and 91 acres, 70 of which he planted as prune, cherry and peach orchards. Frank and his wife then resided in the family home for the rest of their lives. After his death in 1948, the land was parceled out among their children and in 1960 the majority of the land was sold for the Killarney Farms subdivision.

DR. BENJAMIN FRANKLIN HEADEN

*In October 1852, Dr. Benjamin Franklin Headen arrived in Santa Clara and
purchased 61 acres on the outskirts of the township. First grain and then
strawberries and later orchards and vineyards were cultivated on his farm. He was
the first to grow vegetable and flower seeds on a commercial scale, paving the way
for the later development of Santa Clara's seed industry. Dr. Headen began his 20
years of service as a trustee for the College of the Pacific in March 1853, also serving as a trustee of the Methodist Episcopal Church in Santa Clara and in 1868,
the Town Board of Trustees.*

A LUSH SETTING

*Shortly after his arrival, Dr. Benjamin Headen erected an attractive home on the grounds of which he planted flower
seeds he had carried across the plains and young redwood trees brought from the Santa Cruz Mountains. Shown picking flowers in front of their home are his wife Henrietta and daughters, Henrietta and Thomasine.*

THE BRAND NEW TOWN

Drawn four years after the incorporation of the Town of Santa Clara, this

lithograph, the view looking southeast, shows Santa Clara College with

the ex-Mission church and the young town as they appeared in 1856.

Pictured above is the new home Mary had built after Love's death. Pictured (to the right) in this 1865 photo, Mary Bennett exhibits the quality that earned her the reputation of being a strong-willed woman — and Edwin Bryant's description as a "lady of Amazonian proportions."

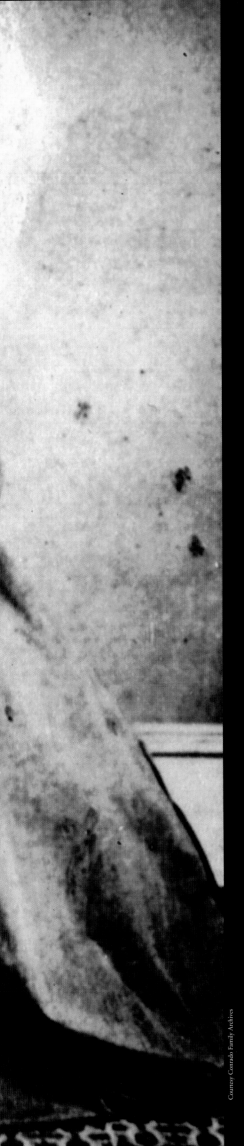

MARY BENNETT
"A MIND OF
HER OWN"

S tanding more than six feet tall and weighing an imposing 300 pounds, Mary McSwain Bennett Love became a legend in her own time during what was probably the most turbulent period in the annals of Santa Clara, the mid-1840s.

She lived in Santa Clara only a little more than two decades, but stories inspired by Mary's actions have continued to be told throughout the subsequent years to the point where she is now considered to be one of the most colorful characters in the history of the area. "While she embodied the characteristics and courage inherent in the women who, for generations, have taken charge of and uprooted their lives in search of a better place to raise their families, she was in her own way unique."[1]

"With almond eyes and sturdy Irish jaw,"[2] Mary Bennett was aptly described by Edwin Bryant when he visited Santa Clara in 1846 as "an American lady of amazonian proportions."[3] She had a personality as commanding as her physical appearance and descriptions of her indicate its complexity. This strong-willed giant of a woman with her deep powerful voice, was portrayed as one who "ruled the roost,"[4] and had "a mind of her own."[5] Depicted as having "an excellent vocabulary which, for sheer artistry, was second to none,"[6] a satirical referral to her extensive vocabulary of profanity, she was also reported as being very affable, humorous, well liked, and hospitable.

One of 13 children, Mary McSwain was born in 1803 in North Carolina.[7] Later this working class family moved to Virginia. Here, at a young age, Mary went to work as a domestic in order to help them out. She eventually obtained employment as a maid in the home of the wealthy Bennett family of Georgia where she met one of their sons, Vardemon. When, against his parent's wishes, he married this tall, then-slim girl of Irish descent, his family practically disowned him. Mary and Vardemon lived in Georgia until after the birth of their first two children, Catherine and Winston, when, unhappy and feeling unjustly treated by his family, Mary persuaded Vardemon to leave. They moved to Tennessee, then to Arkansas where they resided for 10 years. In the early 1840s, as a result of the pillaging of the area by the White Caps,[8] a vigilante-type group, Vardemon became concerned about his family's welfare. So, when Captain Hastings and his group of 150 immigrants came through on their way west, the opportunity was seized to leave with this wagon train. With their eight surviving children (they had lost twins), Mary and Vardemon joined the party and on April 1, 1842, "a beautiful spring day," the Bennett family left their farm in Arkansas. In only one day they had made all the necessary preparations and, taking only their livestock and the necessities for the long trek, they left everything else behind. After a difficult cross-country trip the Hastings-Lovejoy party arrived in Salem, Oregon in October, 1842. The following spring the Bennett family joined those members of the party who had decided to go on to California. After a brief stay in Sacramento, they continued to San Francisco, where Vardemon opened a saloon.

Mary's presence was noticed. W. H. Davis, a leading local businessman, later wrote, "Mrs. Bennett arrived…with her husband and large family of children. I mention her first, as she was unmistakably the head of the family—a large powerful woman, uncultivated, but well-meaning and very industrious. Her word was law and her husband stood in becoming awe of her. Their children were respectively brought up, the family…supported by sewing washing, ironing…I trusted her for goods frequently…She was an honest, good woman, and while not regarded as an equal by the better-cultivated and more aristocratic ladies, (Californio society) she was always pleasantly received in their homes."[9]

In 1845, Mary separated from Vardemon, claiming to the authorities that he failed to support their children. Taking the younger children with her, she went to the Santa Cruz Mountains where she purchased a sawmill and land next to the Zayante Ranch, which was owned by Isaac Graham. Graham, described by Bancroft as "a loud mouthed, unprincipled, profligate and reckless man," had arrived in Alta California around 1833, and two years later set up a crude distillery in Natividad, a few miles east of Watsonville.[10] After meeting Mary's oldest daughter, Catherine, Isaac, then 43 and 22 years older than Catherine, courted and married her. Despite the fact he would treat Catherine "as a queen," there were other times Isaac was physically cruel to her and because of this the union did not set well with Mary. She appealed to Thomas Larkin, the American consul in Monterey, to annul the marriage, an action which earned her Isaac's enmity. However, Catherine stayed with Isaac and two daughters were born to them. In 1850, when his son Jesse, showed up, she learned that Isaac had left a wife and several children in Texas. She was outraged even though Texas law, at that time, considered an absence of seven years a divorce. His first wife had also remarried. Catherine took the children and some of Isaac's hidden stash of gold and left him, escaping on the brig "Emily Browne," which went from Santa Cruz to the Hawaiian Islands. Jesse, believing Mary had taken Catherine and the gold from his father, threatened her, so Mary and her son, Jackson went to Elihu Anthony, the *Alcalde,* (the Local official charged with the maintenance of "order and tranquility") of Branciforte (Santa Cruz), to have Jesse put under bond to keep the peace. At the same time, Jesse went to the Bennett sawmill looking for Mary and there shot and killed Mary's 24-year-old son, Dennis, a shooting which was witnessed by four of her children. When Mary and Jackson arrived, Jesse wounded them and escaped into the Santa Cruz Mountains, never to be found.

Isaac continued searching until he tracked Catherine and their girls to Oregon City, Oregon, where they had moved after leaving the Hawaiian Islands. There he convinced her to reconcile with him, a reconciliation which lasted all of one month. Isaac wanted only his gold and after obtaining that, he left her. Catherine and the girls later returned to Mary's ranch and the marriage was finally annulled in 1852.

Although Mary owned the sawmill and ranch in the Santa Cruz Mountains, she did not operate it, her sons did. In 1846 Mary moved to Santa Clara, taking up residence in an adobe house in the Mission gardens. Here, although Vardemon did not die until 1849, she was known as the "Widow" Bennett.[11]

Controversy quickly followed the arrival of this tenacious and independent woman. On June 5, 1846, Thomas Larkin, in a letter to the *alcalde* at San Jose, "requested protection for Mary from harassment from her husband," and "thanked Father Real (of Mission Santa Clara) for providing her a house in the Mission orchard."[12]

On March 3, 1847, less than a year after Mary's arrival, Father Real felt it necessary to send a letter to John Burton, the San Jose *alcalde,* requesting help in having her removed. In it he wrote:

"…The said Sra. Persistently insists in not vacating the Mission gardens by offering a thousand falsehoods and subterfuges without presenting documents to prove the illegality and injustice of our claim, with which she desires to take possession of a particular proprietorship without respect to the decisions of the first magistrates. This conduct which is so ungrateful of the Sra. Bennett has placed me in the obligation of asking for a new complaint … I have the honor to place this before your judgment. Repeating, I remain your obedient servant.
—Friar Señor Maria del Padre Jesus del Real"[13]

The sheer nerve she later exhibited during the U.S. land commission hearings on her claim to this parcel of land, when she alleged that Father Real "gave her a sowing lot (the Mission garden land) in 1845,"[14] is typical of Mary's pluck and tenacity.

Mary had originally settled on about 60 acres of Mission land but as the town grew, it developed in this area. She had not fenced the land to protect her "rights," so others then "squatted" on the property. Mary soon became perpetually embroiled in some kind of suit, at first battling these squatters (although she had "squatted" herself), then lawyers and money lenders, and later fighting for confirmation of the two tracts of land she claimed. These were not small parcels and quite possibly Mary envisioned how valuable they would be to the growth of the fledgling town of Santa Clara. They totaled 358.51 acres and one tract (Tract I) occupied the area between what is today Saratoga Avenue and Homestead Road. The other tract (Tract II) was located within what became the town limits of Santa Clara. This land had reportedly been granted to Mary by the Mexican government because of her medical assistance during various epidemics and, as she was a skilled midwife, for the aid she provided to the local *Californio* and Indian population whenever a birth was expected. However, like many cover more land than she was entitled to, at one time maintaining her land ran the long way through the town boundaries of the two tracts she claimed. The people in town faced major losses if Mary Bennett's claim was upheld and they protested loudly. A contemporary newspaper article describes the situation:

"From a private letter, we learn that the ordinarily quiet town of Santa Clara is now the scene of excitement caused by the survey of the Mary S. Bennett claim… running north and south with the street that leads from Otterson's Hotel to Forbes' brick building, embracing all the protestant churches, school houses and colleges and, in fact, all the business portion of the town. The citizens have been holding meetings every day since the making of the survey."[15]

However, Mary had a truly remarkable ability to retain her property during a time when legal expenses soared and interest rates on borrowed money ran as high as three per cent a month, which caused many claimants to lose their land while embroiled in the courts.

While she did not receive the full acreage claimed, Mary ended up possessing extensive land holdings in Santa Clara.[16] Tracts I and II were confirmed to her in 1861, but only Tract I (outside the town limits) was eventually patented to her in 1871, three years after her death. She also owned 11 acres within the town limits, the four blocks between Lewis, Fremont, Alviso and Sherman Streets.[17] Mary resided on this latter portion of her property, which had a fine artesian well, and here she raised chickens, geese and turkeys, often providing passing travelers with lodging and meals.

One of these travelers was Harry Love, who had gained fame as captain of the California Rangers, the expedition which had tracked down and killed the notorious bandit Joaquin Murrieta in July 1853, and he was still enjoying this triumph. Captain Love, a powerfully built man who stood six-foot-two, often stopped at

Mary's home when in the area and although he was 16 years younger than Mary, a romance soon blossomed – perhaps Mary's ample size was the attraction for Captain Love, who has been described as a "grizzly bear." In any case, the colorful couple was wed around 1855. Mary, as well known for her "sharp tongue" as for her warm heart, was "used to running her own business and family and objected to Harry having anything to say about either."[18] They battled continuously and spent most of the time separating and making up.

Disaster occurred in 1868. At that time, Mary was separated from Harry Love. She had hired Christian Iverson as a day-laborer and, as she had become very heavy, one of Iverson's tasks was to assist her in and out of her buggy when she drove to San Jose. Harry had become jealous of young Iverson and threatened him many times. Finally, he attempted to ambush Iverson on June 29 and this attempt fatally backfired when Iverson seriously wounded Love in the arm during the encounter. A paragraph in the San Jose Mercury of July 2, 1868, describes what happened: "Captain Love had threatened to kill…(Iverson), who armed himself against possible attack. On…their return home from a trip to San Jose, Mary and the young German were met by Harry Love who, armed with a shotgun, a pistol and a bowie knife, had waited in hiding behind the garden fence at their residence. The second barrel only wounded the German, who was able to get close enough to the fence to fire a bullet point blank into Harry Love's arm near the shoulder." His arm had to be amputated and Harry died later that day either from the effects of the amputation or the chloroform or both."[19]

After Love's death, Mary continued living alone while constructing a new home at 1385 Grant Street.[20] However, she did not live to see it completed. In December, 1868, while visiting the McCusker Ranch

(Catherine was married by then to her second husband, Daniel McCusker, whom she met when he purchased her mother's sawmill in 1852, shortly after the annulment of her marriage to Isaac) Mary fell ill. It is quite possible she was the victim of smallpox, which was spreading in epidemic proportions throughout Santa Clara at that time. She died at the age of 65.[21] Mary McSwain Bennett Love was buried at the Pioneer Cemetery in Freedom near Watsonville and the colorful career of this indomitable woman was over.

A century and a half have passed since Mary Bennett arrived in Santa Clara but this self-willed woman who took her life in her own hands and successfully competed in a "man's world" gained a notoriety in her time which continues to this day. As a result, who she really was and what she really did has been shrouded in layers of legends and rumors.

For example, recollections about events which occurred during the battle of Santa Clara in January 1847, state that she berated Joseph Aram and the American men at the Mission for their "lack of courage and participation."[22] It is said that, "She waltzed back and forth in front of the Mission yelling orders to the men at the top of her voice…and, grabbing up a large bone…rushed up to a man who had refused to fight…and shouted 'take that you puppy, and go out there and bat the brains out of some Mexican or I'll use it on you.'"[23] However, while Mary was indeed outspoken with a reputation for using profanity, she had an affable relationship with the *Californio/*Mexican population, several of whom she had helped when they needed medical care. Given this relationship, it is highly doubtful that she would have shown such animosity toward them. Also, most of the descriptions of what transpired at the battle have proved to be highly inaccurate and written from a cultural bias, such as Aram's statement that, "The

Americans were cool and determined and anxious to get as near as possible" and "The Spaniards…preferred to fight at a good distance from our lines; they seemed to dread the whizzing of our bullets."[24] Indeed, these American immigrants looked askance on efforts made to aid them during the winter of 1846 by George Bellomy, who had immigrated to Oregon and California in the same party as the Bennett family, because he was married to Maria Bernal, a *Californio* woman. Moreover, by the time these recollections were written, Mary's colorful life, land claims, and disastrous marriage to Harry Love had caused many people in Santa Clara to view her behavior in a very dubious light, crediting her with several outrageous actions.

Her descendants however, have seen Mary and her life in a very different manner, remembering her sense of humor and friendliness and applauding her independence and spirit. Her great-granddaughter, Mabel Dorn Early, stated in a 1967 interview, "Do not get the idea that Mary was an overbearing, quarrelsome woman. Grandmother (Catherine) always said that she was fond of joking, very friendly and that everyone liked her."[25] And at his mother's 90th birthday Paul Conrado, Mary Bennett's great-great-great grandson, said, "Mary was part of the stuff of which the new state was made" and "the spirit of this pioneer women continues in the succession of ladies." From Mary to her daughter Catherine Bennett McCusker, to her daughter Josephine McCusker Dorn, to her daughter Mabel Dorn Hirst Early, who was an advocate for women's rights and having passed the Bar in her thirties, ran for Police Court Judge in San Francisco following WWI, to his own mother Annabel (Anne Mabel) Hirst Conrado, who, when she lost her husband at a young age raised her seven children alone and although deaf did volunteer work until she was in her nineties, it can truly be said that "the family is a line of women, not a line of men."

" ...STORES, CHURCHES... COTTAGES IN THE MIDST OF ORCHARDS."

The Town of Santa Clara was incorporated on July 5, 1852 with the approval of the State Legislature, and on July 24 the first Town Board of Trustees, made up of Fielding Laird (Lard), S.S. Johnson, A.D. Hight, Fletcher Cooper and Riley Moultry (Moultrie) assembled for its initial session. Laird was elected president of the Board, C.W. Adams, clerk pro tem, Abraham Madan, assessor and William Fosgate, marshall.[1] With the exception of Moultry, who had arrived in late 1846, all these men were American immigrants who had settled in Santa Clara less then four years before their election to the Board.

In order to establish an American form of town government, structuring laws of procedure and adopting ordinances was the chief business of the Board. The first of these ordinances focused on the regulation of public behavior and addressed breach of the peace, obstruction of streets, and horse racing.

Meeting irregularly, some times in the "little brick school," sometimes in the members' places of business and homes, the members of the Board of Trustees appeared to hold their positions in light regard as most of them left office to travel — many times without the formality of submitting resignations. The early records of Santa Clara list at least half a dozen elections during the first couple of years.[2] Along with the lack of a committed leadership, the young

Peter J. Riley Photo, c. 1922, Santa Clara Woman's Club Archives

CRIME AND PUNISHMENT

Constructed of adobe with walls two feet thick, this two room building was located at the corner of Jackson and Harrison Streets and served as a jail for both the Mission and early American periods in Santa Clara history. One of the rooms had no windows and was the jail; the other was used as a kitchen. The floor consisted of heavy planks and prisoners were handcuffed to a number of rings secured to the floor and the building walls. After the property was sold to Lewis Gardner in 1855, its use as a jail was discontinued and it became a storeroom and woodshed. The building was demolished in April, 1922, but not before newspaperman Peter J. Riley dashed between the wreckers and the adobe and took this photograph.

municipality struggled to institute a stable financial system as illustrated by an interview in the San Jose Daily Mercury of April 9, 1904 by the first treasurer of the Town of Santa Clara, Thomas Brothers, in which he said: "… in those days there was very little money in the treasury." Brothers went on to recall an instance when a circus came to town and a license tax of $20 was charged the circus people. "The money remained in the treasury for some time and the trustees did not know what to do with it, so one night they all turned out and disposed of it in an oyster supper."

The image of "the garden spot of the United States" had been applied to California and Santa Clara County since 1846, when Lansford W. Hastings, a zeal-

ous real estate promoter, published a book entitled "The Emigrant's Guide to Oregon and California." In the book he called California a place of "perpetual spring" where no "noxious miasmatic effluvia" existed, and the rapidity of agricultural development in Santa Clara seemed to justify this belief. By 1854, only eight years after the first large overland group of American immigrants had arrived in Santa Clara, orchards and vineyards had been developed to the point where there was a market for 15,000 fruit trees and a wide variety of grape stock.[3] Entwined with the growth of agriculture was the highly complex question of land ownership, and land titles in the Santa Clara Valley were to remain in a state of uncertainty during the 1850s and early 1860s as residents waited for the outcome of the United States Land Commission's decisions.[4] Nonetheless, the Town of Santa Clara continued to expand, with the Town's Board of Trustees repeatedly adopting ordinances to deal with the resultant issues raised by that growth. Visiting in 1859 after a ten year absence, Bayard Taylor was struck by the "checkerwork of new streets — brick stores, churches, smiling cottages in the midst of gardens and orchards."[5]

Prior to the arrival of American settlers, Catholicism was the only religion practiced in Santa Clara. However, in order to meet the religious needs of the young American community, Protestant churches were quickly established. The Methodists were the first Protestant denomination to be organized (1847), and in 1851-53 they constructed an adobe church in town. Also, in 1851, the Baptist and other Protestant churches were organized.

From the earliest days, public safety was an issue of major concern. Shortly after his arrival in 1846, William Haun was appointed alcalde (chief governing official of a Spanish town) and he also acted as jailer for Santa Clara. The same two-room adobe structure with walls two feet thick that had served the Mission as a jail was used for that purpose once again. Located on the southwest corner of Jackson and Harrison Streets, this structure continued to serve as the town jail until the mid 1850s when its use was discontinued.

The Gold Rush had brought a lawless element to the area and problems with "squatters" had risen, so in 1851 a group of Santa Clara men organized a "Vigilance Committee."[6] As the government gained stability the need for the vigilantes passed and they were disbanded. After incorporation, the Town government included a marshal, whose responsibilities included not only keeping the peace and enforcing the laws which had been passed, but several other duties, from rounding up stray hogs to street repairs.[7]

Starting in 1850, the position of town constable existed (a position similar to that of today's deputy sheriff). He acted as a bailiff of the court and was responsible for serving the writs issued by the township justice of the peace.[8] Throughout the years Santa Clara usually had two constables who worked closely with the town marshal and many of the marshals also served as constable, sometimes filling both offices simultaneously.

Before the formation of the first volunteer fire company, each home kept several water buckets and fire was fought by a bucket brigade. In 1855, after a disastrous fire had occurred, a number of citizens met and organized the Tiger Engine Co., whose initial equipment consisted of an old hose cart and some buckets. The next year, having raised the necessary funds, an engine and hose was purchased, and after its arrival in Santa Clara in July, 1856, Tiger Engine Co. officially changed its name to the Columbian Engine Co. No.1 in honor of the San Francisco company from whom the engine had been purchased. Next, they purchased a lot on Washington Street near Lexington and built a fire station on it.

In order to prosper it quickly became evident that a regular means of transporting people and goods was crucial. In the fall of 1849, John Whistman established the first stage service in California, a nine-hour run between San Jose and San Francisco. However, by July, 1851, this was still the only means of land transportation to San Francisco with service to Monterey only available twice a week. The 1850s saw the construction of toll roads over the Santa Cruz Mountains. A mountain route was established between Santa Cruz and San Jose in 1857 and the following year there was a stage route on the San Jose-Soquel Turnpike.[9] After the turnpike opened on October 16, 1858, the Cameron House and the Union Hotel in Santa Clara, both operated by John Cameron, served as stopping places for the Santa Cruz stages. There

CAMERON HOUSE.

JOHN H. CAMERON, Proprietor. Franklin Street, SANTA CLARA. THE ABOVE HOUSE IS NOW OPEN for the reception of guests. It has all the modern improvements usually found in THE BEST HOTELS. It has splendidly furnished suits [sic.] of rooms for families and is not excelled–equalled–by any house outside of San Francisco. A coach will be at the Depot on the arrival of each train to convey passengers and their luggage to the Hotel. JOHN H. CAMERON, Prop. Santa Clara, May 1st, 1867.

(The Pacific Sentinel, Santa Cruz, California, May 11, 1867).

THE UNION HOTEL,

kept by Cameron, at Santa Clara is well worth the patronage of the public. The "Overland Stages" from Santa Cruz stop there, and the proprietor of the Hotel has a high reputation for a good table, good beds, and for courtesy and attention. Try him.

(The Pacific Sentinel, Santa Cruz, California, November 13, 1858.)

THE BEST HOTELS

Located on the southeast corner of Franklin and Main Streets, John Cameron's Union Hotel (originally operated by Appleton and Ainslee) and Cameron House provided accommodations for travelers, first by stage and then by train as shown by the above advertisements.

breakfast was served to the passengers who arrived from Santa Cruz on the overnight stage that connected with a ship at Alviso destined for San Francisco.[10]

In 1852, when the first county supervisors were elected, farmers between the redwoods and the Bay petitioned them for a new road by which to deliver their wheat, hay and lumber to the flour mills and to the port of Alviso. Haste was urged because the "prairie was rapidly being fenced and land prices were going up."[11] The board was agreeable, although the farmers were upset at the tax hike involved.[12] Today, Lawrence Expressway roughly follows the old route of Lawrence Station Road, the first road built to specifically accommodate the transportation of agricultural products.

Between Santa Clara and San Jose, the chief link was The Alameda. Originally it cost $5 to hire a hack, but by the late 1850s stagecoaches were running on The Alameda between the two towns. In 1858, William Fitts started working for the first service, and two years later established his own line.

The bumps and mud-holes on The Alameda necessitated constant and costly repairs.[13] Once consid-

Located on the southwest corner of Monroe and Franklin Streets, this structure was originally constructed in the 1850s as the home of Robert Seydel. By 1882 with Franklin Street's development into Santa Clara's main commercial street and trolley service then extended to Lincoln Street, it had become the Hotel Glenwood.

Irving Cabral Collections, Santa Clara Historic Archives

ered a boon, the willow trees that lined the road had grown to more than 40 feet in height and, because of the shade they created, became a problem by keeping the road boggy in the rainy season when the surrounding open land had dried out. In 1862, Hiram Shartzer of Santa Clara offered to improve conditions by making The Alameda a toll road. He graded the thoroughfare, filled in holes and installed toll gates that charged 10 cents for buggies and $1 for stages. Displeased at having to pay passage on a road that remained a quagmire in the winter, people welcomed the advent of horse-drawn railway cars six years later. For a dime passengers could glide down The Alameda on a narrow-gauge railroad which local boosters claimed was "the west's first interurban horse car line." However, for five years or more after the first horse cars came, stagecoaches still were seen on The Alameda.

Although it had become easier and faster for people to travel, the high costs and inefficiency of utilizing the Port of Alviso affected industrial growth. For a mobile society, with its cash-based economy that relied on the sending and receiving of goods, another means of transportation was necessary. Again, sights were set on building a railroad.[14] This time the Santa Clara Tannery

and the Knowles Pottery Company, in an effort to reach larger markets and increase their profits, allied with the College of Santa Clara to support its construction.[15] On August 18, 1860, the San Francisco and San Jose Railroad was incorporated, and on January 17, 1864, regular service between San Francisco and San Jose started with two trains running each way on Sundays and one round trip on weekdays. It was the second railroad to be completed in California.

The political influence exerted on the S.F. and S.J. Railroad Company by the Santa Clara College Board of Trustees was a decisive factor in having a passenger depot constructed in Santa Clara, one of two "way depots" built between San Francisco and San Jose and only three miles from the railroad terminus in San Jose.[16] The depot needed to be near the existing stage routes so the parcel chosen for it was at the junction of Benton and Franklin Streets. Prior to 1864, horse-drawn wagons transported fruit produce from the orchards along Benton Street to the port of Alviso for shipment to San Francisco and Oakland. Franklin Street connecting to The Alameda was the main road for goods and travelers between Santa Clara and San Jose.[17]

The San Francisco and San Jose Railroad provided more convenient local shipping than the cumbersome wagons connecting Santa Clara and Alviso, and drastically reduced the amount of stage traffic because of their improved speed, comfort and lower cost.[18] While road traffic outside of Santa Clara was significantly reduced, within the Town itself, Benton and Franklin Streets continued to play an important local role and Franklin Street became the main commercial street in the "downtown" section.

A tremendous increase in property values occurred with the improvements in transportation and the economic growth made possible by the railroad. Its construction resulted in a variety of fruit-related businesses developing within the township as the proximity of the depot to the orchards made Santa Clara a prime location for them, thus enabling the Town to play an important role in the growing fruit industry.[19] (When the transcontinental railroad was completed in 1869, the first load of fresh pears from California was shipped east by Levi Gould, a Santa Clara orchardist.)

Education continued to be a priority as the Town grew. Schools were constructed by public institutions and by religious organizations. In 1853, the Methodists established The Female Institute, a school of higher education for girls, located on the southeast corner of Jackson and Liberty (Homestead) Streets. As the population increased, in order to serve the areas outside of the Town limits, one-room schools, Millikin and Braly in 1855 and Jefferson in 1861, were built. Within the town, The Sisters of Notre Dame established Notre Dame Academy, a day school for girls, in 1864. They purchased James Alexander Forbes' house (the first brick house built in Santa Clara) eight years later to accommodate growing enrollment.[20] In 1867, Santa Clara Grammar School was opened.

JAMES W. EASTIN

The legislation which created California's original 27 counties in 1850 also provided for a Court of Sessions for each county, which was authorized to "divide the county into townships." That year, the Santa Clara County Court of Sessions created five townships within Santa Clara County, including the Township of Santa Clara, with each township authorized to have two justices of the peace. After the Town of Santa Clara was incorporated in 1852, there existed within the County two similarly named entities, the Township of Santa Clara and within that, the Town of Santa Clara, each entitled to its own separate court system. One of the first two Township Justices elected was James W. Eastin, who had come to California in 1847. He served as a Justice of the Peace of the Township of Santa Clara from 1852 to 1857, and also served on the Town of Santa Clara Board of Trustees in 1853.

TREES FOR SALE

Commodore Robert F. Stockton, having retired from his military and political career, purchased Rancho El Potrero de Santa Clara in 1847 from James Alexander Forbes and in 1852 had apple, peach, pear, nectarine and apricot root stock sent from Massachusetts for the purpose of establishing a nursery of his own on this land. Two years later, he advertised 15,000 fruit trees for sale along with grape stock and strawberry plants. Early nurserymen like the Commodore gave Santa Clara its start as a community whose economic base was orchards and vineyards by providing farmers with the needed fruit trees and grape stock to begin the transformation from raising grain.

Fruit Trees at Auction.

15,000 FRUIT TREES, from Two to Three Years old, will be offered for sale at auction on the 12TH DECEMBER, at 10 o'clock, A. M., on the Stockton Rancho, on the Almaden, or road leading from the city of San Jose to Santa Clara, Santa Clara County.

Those wishing to purchase large, healthy and vigorous trees will do well to call and look at these trees before purchasing elsewhere, *as they are all positively to be sold.*

The following comprise some of the varieties:

APPLES THREE YEARS OLD.—Early Strawberry, Swaar, Baldwin, Sweet Bough, W. King, Fall Pippin, Seek no further, Wagoner, Rhode Island Greening, Gravenstein, Juneating, Early Joe, Golden Sweet, Newtown Pippin, Northern Spy, Roxbury Russet, Priestly.

APPLES TWO YEARS OLD.—Early Harvest, Ladies' Sweeting, R. I. Greening, Northern Spy, Swaar, Wagoner, Spitzenburg, Sweet Bough, Baldwin, &c.

PEARS TWO YEARS OLD.—Winter Nellis, Bartlet, Beurre diel, Dearborn Seedling, Duchess de Angouleme, Vicar of Winkfield, President, Virgalieu Onondago.

PLUMS.—Bleekers Green Gage, Red Magnum Bonum.

PEACH TREES.—12,000 Peach Trees, two years old.

APRICOT TREES.—4,000 Apricot Trees, two years old, several of the choicest varieties, and will bear the coming season if carefully transplanted.

FOREIGN GRAPES.—Muscat Blanc Hatif, Black Morocco, Joslins St. Albans, Black Prince, Black Corinthian, Frank Renthal, De La Palestine, Buist's superb, Fromeatal, White Frontignac, Deacon's superb.

Will bear the following year if carefully moved: Early Crawford, Old Mixon, Early York, Jacques Rareripe, Morris White, Red-cheeked Melacaton, Grosse Mignone, Honest John, &c.

Strawberry Plants of choice varieties.

Green-house Plants, &c.

Terms, Cash on Day of Sale.

20   JAS. F. KENNEDY, Agent.

The California Farmer, Lorie Garcia Historical Collection

Santa Clara Historic Archives

TO GUARD MY EVERY NEIGHBOR AND PROTECT HIS PROPERTY

Meeting at the Union Hotel on October 5, 1855, a number of citizens formed Santa Clara's first organized fire company, the Tiger Engine Company, with a dilapidated hose cart and a few buckets constituting their equipment. This situation was rectified the following year when the volunteers were able to raise enough money to purchase an engine and hose.

COLUMBIAN ENGINE COMPANY NO. 1 AND TANNER HOSE CO.

When the Tiger Engine Company purchased new equipment in 1856, it changed its name to Columbian Engine Company No.1 in honor of the San Francisco company from which the new engine had come. Uniforms consisted of a red shirt, black pants, blue cap trimmed with a red and black patent leather front piece, a black belt with gold lettering and a metal badge worn on the left breast. In this 1875 photo, the men on the left with the jackets are from Tanner Hose Company.

WILLIAM FITTS

In 1858, William "Billy" Fitts was hired to drive the omnibus which ran on The
Alameda, from the Cameron House in Santa Clara to the Auzerais House in San Jose.
Two years later he started a line of his own, which ran for nine years until the completion
of the San Jose & Santa Clara Horse Railroad put him out of business. Following this, he
served as Santa Clara County jailer and in 1876 was elected Santa Clara Town Marshal,
a position he held for four consecutive terms. Fitts returned to the transportation business
in 1881 as superintendent of the S.J. & S.C. horse line, a job he held until 1890 when
electrification of the railroad eliminated the horse line. While he was driving the omnibus,
he met Dolores Pinedo, daughter of Lorenzo Pinedo, (grantee of Rancho Las Uvas) and
Carmen Berryessa de Pinedo, who rode the omnibus line to the school run by the sisters of
Notre Dame Convent in San Jose. They married in 1864.

MAJOR JOHN A. COOK

Having come to San Jose while representing San Diego County in the State Legislature in 1850-51, John Cook settled in Santa Clara and, a widower, married Jane Fulkerson.

Mary (Anthony) Pascoe, Bea Lichtenstein Collection

Mary (Anthony) Pascoe, Bea Lichtenstein Collection

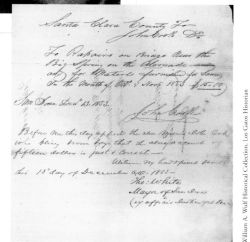

William A. Wulf Historical Collection, Los Gatos Historian

MAJOR JOHN COOK'S HOME

In the summer of 1853 the Cooks built a home just off The Alameda on Deep Springs Lake, a body of water which had served as the mission pozo or well. Later the area became known as Cook's Pond or Cook's Grove and was used for events such as Santa Clara College graduations and the celebration of the nation's centennial in 1876.

REPAIRS

With The Alameda the major road between Santa Clara and San Jose, John Cook took care of the maintenance of a bridge over it, on or near his property. This December, 1853 receipt indicates the following reimbursement: "Santa Clara County To John Cook – To Repairs on Bridge near the Big Spring on the Alemade (Alameda) and for materials furnished for same in the month of Oct. & Nov. 1853…$15.00."

NATHANIEL WHEELER COOK

In 1857, Nathaniel Cook and his family moved to Santa Clara, where his father, Major John Cook, had previously settled. Nathaniel became one of the first engineers employed by the steam flour mill and later its part owner. He was one of the early Township Justices of the Peace and also served as foreman of the County Grand Jury.

NATHANIEL WHEELER COOK'S HOME

Nathaniel, his wife, Eliza Jane, and their four children lived in a Gothic-style home located at Lewis and Lafayette Streets. circa 1880 Santa Clara.

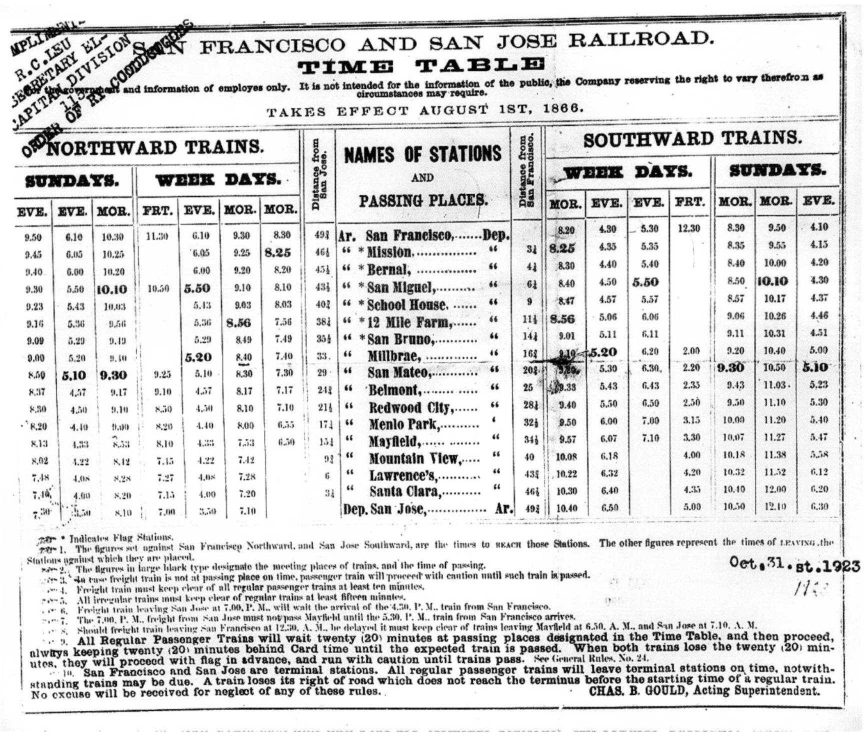

R.C. LEU

CAPITAL DIVISION

SAN FRANCISCO AND SAN JOSE RAILROAD.

TIME TABLE

For the government and information of employes only. It is not intended for the information of the public, the Company reserving the right to vary therefrom as circumstances may require.

TAKES EFFECT AUGUST 1ST, 1866.

NORTHWARD TRAINS. Sundays. EVE.	Sundays. EVE.	Sundays. MOR.	Week Days. FRT.	Week Days. EVE.	Week Days. MOR.	Week Days. MOR.	Distance from San Jose.	NAMES OF STATIONS AND PASSING PLACES.	Distance from San Francisco.	SOUTHWARD TRAINS. Week Days. MOR.	Week Days. EVE.	Week Days. EVE.	Week Days. FRT.	Sundays. MOR.	Sundays. MOR.	Sundays. EVE.
9.50	6.10	10.30	11.30	6.10	9.30	8.30	49¾	Ar. San Francisco,.......Dep.		8.20	4.30	5.30	12.30	8.30	9.50	4.10
9.45	6.05	10.25		6.05	9.25	**8.25**	46½	" * Mission,............... "	3¼	**8.25**	4.35	5.35		8.35	9.55	4.15
9.40	6.00	10.20		6.00	9.20	8.20	45½	" * Bernal,............... "	4¼	8.30	4.40	5.40		8.40	10.00	4.20
9.30	5.50	**10.10**	10.50	**5.50**	9.10	8.10	43½	" * San Miguel,......... "	6¼	8.40	4.50	**5.50**		8.50	**10.10**	4.30
9.23	5.43	10.03		5.43	9.03	8.03	40¾	" * School House, ... "	9	8.47	4.57	5.57		8.57	10.17	4.37
9.16	5.36	9.56		5.36	**8.56**	7.56	38¼	" * 12 Mile Farm,...... "	11½	**8.56**	5.06	6.06		9.06	10.26	4.46
9.09	5.29	9.49		5.29	8.49	7.49	35½	" * San Bruno,.......... "	14¼	9.01	5.11	6.11		9.11	10.31	4.51
9.00	5.20	9.40		**5.20**	8.40	7.40	33.	" Millbrae,............ "	16¾	9.10	**5.20**	6.20	2.00	9.20	10.40	5.00
8.50	**5.10**	**9.30**	9.25	5.10	8.30	7.30	29	" San Mateo,........... "	20¾	[illegible]	5.30	6.30	2.20	**9.30**	10.50	**5.10**
8.37	4.57	9.17	9.10	4.57	8.17	7.17	24¾	" Belmont,........... "	25	9.33	5.43	6.43	2.35	9.43	11.03	5.23
8.30	4.50	9.10	8.50	4.50	8.10	7.10	21½	" Redwood City,...... "	28¼	9.40	5.50	6.50	2.50	9.50	11.10	5.30
8.20	4.40	9.00	8.20	4.40	8.00	6.55	17¼	" Menlo Park,......... "	32½	9.50	6.00	7.00	3.15	10.00	11.20	5.40
8.13	4.33	8.53	8.10	4.33	7.53	6.50	15¼	" Mayfield,........... "	34½	9.57	6.07	7.10	3.30	10.07	11.27	5.47
8.02	4.22	8.12	7.45	4.22	7.42		9¾	" Mountain View,.... "	40	10.08	6.18		4.00	10.18	11.38	5.58
7.48	4.08	8.28	7.27	4.08	7.28		6	" Lawrence's,.......... "	43¾	10.22	6.32		4.20	10.32	11.52	6.12
7.40	4.00	8.20	7.15	4.00	7.20		3¼	" Santa Clara,......... "	46½	10.30	6.40		4.35	10.40	12.00	6.20
7.30	3.50	8.10	7.00	3.50	7.10			Dep. San Jose,.............. Ar.	49¾	10.40	6.50		5.00	10.50	12.10	6.30

* Indicates Flag Stations.

1. The figures set against San Francisco Northward, and San Jose Southward, are the times to REACH those Stations. The other figures represent the times of LEAVING the Stations against which they are placed.
2. The figures in large black type designate the meeting places of trains, and the time of passing.
3. In case freight train is not at passing place on time, passenger train will proceed with caution until such train is passed.
4. Freight train must keep clear of all regular passenger trains at least ten minutes.
5. All irregular trains must keep clear of regular trains at least fifteen minutes.
6. Freight train leaving San Jose at 7.00, P. M., will wait the arrival of the 4.30, P. M., train from San Francisco.
7. The 7.00, P. M., freight from San Jose must not pass Mayfield until the 5.30, P. M., train from San Francisco arrives.
8. Should freight train leaving San Francisco at 12.30, A. M., be delayed it must keep clear of trains leaving Mayfield at 6.50, A. M., and San Jose at 7.10, A. M.
9. All Regular Passenger Trains will wait twenty (20) minutes at passing places designated in the Time Table, and then proceed, always keeping twenty (20) minutes behind Card time until the expected train is passed. When both trains lose the twenty (20) minutes, they will proceed with flag in advance, and run with caution until trains pass. See General Rules, No. 24.
10. San Francisco and San Jose are terminal stations. All regular passenger trains will leave terminal stations on time, notwithstanding trains may be due. A train loses its right of road which does not reach the terminus before the starting time of a regular train. No excuse will be received for neglect of any of these rules.

CHAS. B. GOULD, Acting Superintendent.

Oct. 31. st. 1923

Edward Peterman Museum of Railroad History, South Bay Historical Railroad Society

ALL ABOARD

Starting in January 1864, with two daily trains each way and additional service offered on the freight train which had passenger cars attached to its rear, the San Francisco and San Jose RR would offer three daily passenger trains between San Francisco and San Jose by August, 1866.

THE DEPOT

The Santa Clara Passenger Depot was relocated across the railroad tracks and attached to the Freight House in 1877, as shown in this 1912 Southern Pacific inventory photo. Considered the oldest continually operating depot west of the Mississippi River, it has been virtually unchanged since its construction in 1863-64.

Edward Peterman Museum of Railroad History, South Bay Historical Railroad Society

THE FIRST SANTA CLARA PEARS

Alice Hare Photo, Clyde Arbuckle Collection

On October 12, 1869, pioneer orchardist Levi Ames Gould shipped the first carload of fresh fruit from California to the eastern states. This shipment consisted of pears he had raised in his Santa Clara orchards.

NOT QUITE COEDUCATION

Although when the Methodists had established the University of the Pacific in 1851 it was decided that "the College should be open to such females as may desire to pursue a college course," it was not until 1853 that the female department of the College officially organized and became known as the Female Collegiate Institute. Operated separately from the Male Department, this department had its own building with separate classes taught by its own faculty. The women students occupied this building located on Main Street between Lexington and Liberty (Homestead) Streets until 1871, when the Female Collegiate Institute left Santa Clara and moved with the Male Department to its new location at College Park.

MILLIKIN SCHOOL

Largest of the four rural schools, Millikin School was originally a small whitewashed one-room redwood cabin which was moved to the corner of Pomeroy Avenue and Homestead Road. There, a second larger building was built to replace it.

THE SECOND MILLIKIN SCHOOL

The second Millikin School was a two-story structure with two rooms on the first floor and an auditorium with stairs to it on the second floor. After Millikin School District became part of the Jefferson Union School District, a Yugoslav social club bought the building and re-named it Napredak Hall.

Ella Sharp and her class are shown seated in front of the original Jefferson School, a one-room, wooden schoolhouse which sat on a two-acre plot of land, donated by Mr. Kifer, which was located on Kifer Road on the northeast bank of San Tomas Creek. This school served as a public school continuously until 1926, when it became a special school for Japanese children, a use which lasted until World War II.

George and Lois Brown Family Collection. c.1900

Santa Clara Unified School District Archives, Don Callejon

JEFFERSON UNION SCHOOL

In 1926, a public election resulted in the formation of the Jefferson Union School District, and by the fall of 1927 the newly constructed Jefferson School, located at the corner of Lawrence Station Road and Monroe Street, opened.

SANTA CLARA GRAMMAR SCHOOL

By 1866, growing enrollment necessitated the construction of a larger school, and in 1867 Santa Clara Grammar School, located on two and a quarter acres situated between Harrison, Fremont, Monroe and Madison Streets, replaced the "Little Brick School." which was located on Lexington, now the site of St. Clare's Church. This two-story structure, 80 feet square, contained eight rooms and by 1895 an annex containing five rooms had been constructed next to it.

Clyde Arbuckle Collection, Jim Arbuckle

Santa Clara Historic Archives

GRAMMAR SCHOOL
CLASSROOM OF 1901

Enrollment had grown over the years, until by 1900 the school census showed 940 children (478 boys and 462 girls) were enrolled. The school was very crowded, but the opening of the new high school building in 1905 helped alleviate the situation. Santa Clara Grammar School continued in use until 1913, when it was replaced by Fremont School.

A WAY TO COMMUNICATE

In April, 1870 a newsletter called the School Reporter was initiated by the Santa Clara Public School, to facilitate communication "that would reach every one interested in our school." It proposed "1st, To publish the monthly standings of all our scholars," "2nd. To publish compositions written by our scholars," and "3rd, To publish such educational items…which we think of sufficient importance to be placed before you."

Santa Clara Unified School District Archives, Don Callejon

AN ACADEMY FOR GIRLS

Mary Certa, Charles D. South Family Collection

NOTRE DAME ACADEMY ORCHESTRAL STUDENTS

Leonard McKay's Clyde Arbuckle Collection

Instruction in cultural as well as academic subjects was received by the young ladies who attended Notre Dame Academy.

Having founded Notre Dame College in San Jose in 1851, the Sisters of Notre Dame in January, 1864 extended their work to open an academy for girls in Santa Clara. First called St. Mary's, then The Academy of Our Lady of Angels and finally Notre Dame Academy, for the first eight years the school was housed in a one-room frame house. When James Alexander Forbes' house was put up for sale in 1872, Father Accolti of Santa Clara College felt that the mansion would be an ideal site for the academy and suggested the sisters purchase it to accommodate the growing academy. They bought the building in October of that year for $8000. Classes were held in the parlors and four small rooms were converted into two large classrooms. Afterwards, they added a second story above the classrooms to accommodate a boarding school. A small wooden building served as a home for the sisters, who had been commuting between Santa Clara and their San Jose convent. In 1874 a large frame building was constructed for the boarding students. In 1924, Notre Dame Academy for girls and St. Joseph's School for boys were united to form St. Clare's School.

SOLEDAD ORTEGA DE ARGUELLO

María de la Soledad de Ortega y Lopez was the wife of Luís Antonio Arguello y Moraga. The last Spanish and first Mexican comandante of the Presidio de San Francisco, her husband was also the first native born governor of California in 1823-25. His father, José Dario Arguello, served as the Presidio Comandante from 1787 to 1806 and had been one of the last Spanish governors of California. Soledad's father, José Ortega, was with the Portolá Expedition in 1769, when the expedition discovered San Francisco Bay.

JOSÉ RAMON ARGUELLO

José Ramon Arguello, son of Soledad and Luís Antonio Arguello, was prominent in the early life of Santa Clara. Educated in Monterey, as a young man he had been in the mercantile business in Mexico City. Then, in 1846, he returned to California to take care of the family interests on their Rancho Las Pulgas in San Mateo County. After being forced to sell off the horses and cattle, which were being stolen by squatters who occupied the rancho land, he returned to Santa Clara where he lived until his death at age 48 in 1876.

ISABEL ALVISO DE ARGUELLO

In 1851, José Ramon Arguello married Isabel Alviso at Mission Santa Clara. She also came from a family that was among the first Spanish arrivals to this area of Alta California. Her grandfather, Ygnacio Alviso, along with his mother and sister, were members of the Juan Bautista de Anza 1775-76 expedition to San Francisco.

LUÍS ANTONIO GONZAGA TRANQUILLINO ARGUELLO

Luís Antonio Gonzaga Tranquillino, José Ramon's brother, was the youngest child of Soledad and Luís Antonio Arguello, born four months after the death of his illustrious father. Like his brother, this son of a family often mentioned as the cream of Californio society, was well educated and was later involved in commercial pursuits with the Americans.

ANGELA BERRYESSA DE ARGUELLO

In 1852, Luís Antonio G. T. Arguello married Angela Berryessa, the daughter of José Ygnacio Berryessa of the New Almaden Berryessa family. They later joined Soledad and José Ramon and his family in the Arguello home, located on the northeast corner of Santa Clara and Main Streets. Here they raised 11 children.

When Soledad Ortega de Arguello returned to Santa Clara in 1857, for $1000 she purchased half a city block which fronted 300 feet on Main Street, and extended 150 feet on Santa Clara Street. A house built by Samuel Scott already existed on the property, and it was incorporated into the rear of the new addition built to accommodate the large family that would reside here. While Soledad moved into José Ramon's new home after its construction, Luís Antonio and his family continued living in this home and in her will Soledad bequeathed it to him. Although today converted into apartments, the house still stands at 1085 Santa Clara Street, its exterior nearly intact.

LUÍS ANTONIO ARGUELLO HOME

JOSÉ RAMON ARGUELLO HOME

After José Ramon Arguello constructed a fine mansion in the 1860s on the northwest corner of Santa Clara and Washington Streets for his wife Isabel and their growing family, his mother Soledad, also moved in, and continued to live with them until her death in 1874.

MARIANO MALARIN

Mariano Malarin was the eldest son of a politically prominent Monterey family when the city was the capitol of Alta California. Elected a member of the California State Assembly in 1859, and re-elected in 1860, he married Isadora Pacheco and they lived in Casa Pacheco in Monterey. In the mid-1860s they moved to Santa Clara, building their new house on the southeast corner of Washington and Santa Clara Streets near the homes of their relatives, the Fatjos and Arguellos. Mariano supervised the family's extensive land holdings in the Salinas Valley, was a member of the San Jose Bar, and president of the San Jose Safe Deposit Bank.

Leonardo Barbieri Painting, 1852-53. De Sassait Museum

ISADORA LOLA (PACHECO) MALARIN

Leonardo Barbieri Painting, 1852. DeSassait Museum

Isadora Pacheco was the daughter of Francisco Perez Pacheco, who included Rancho San Luis Gonzaga in the Pacheco Pass area among his land holdings, which totaled more than 150,000 acres. At the time of her marriage to Mariano Malarin in 1859, Isadora was Francisco's only surviving child and his heiress.

"ALL THE CONVENIENCES OF A MODERN TOWN..."

During the 1860s, the structure of the Town's government was modified in order to adapt to the changing needs. In 1862, Santa Clara was reincorporated with a new charter. In 1866, when the first official survey was made, reincorporation with charter changes occurred again. (Reincorporation would occur again in 1872.)

Other events in the 1860s also had a role in influencing the young municipality's early years. While the Civil War was far distant, life in Santa Clara was not isolated from its effects. Although California had elected to stay with the Union during the conflict, southern sentiment ran high in the young state and with several residents of Santa Clara. A large proportion of the early Americans immigrating to Santa Clara had southern roots and maintained their familial ties. They belonged to a the branch of the Methodist Church known as the Southern Methodist Church. For many members of the community the emotional impact of this war would be deeply felt for years.[1]

Santa Clara Historic Archives

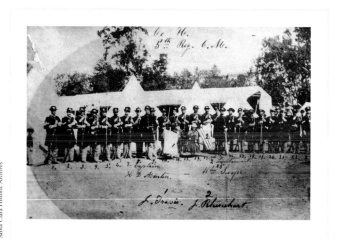

CIVIL WAR UNIT

The members of Santa Clara Co. H, Fifth Regiment gather with Captain H. L. Menton and Lieutenant William Swope. The children holding flags in the center front are J. Travis and J. Rheinhart.

Besides changes effected by man, nature played a role in altering the face of Santa Clara. Beginning in September, 1862, a series of moderate to strong earthquakes struck in areas traversed by the San Andreas Fault, from San Juan Bautista to Eureka, increasing in frequency as the months passed. By mid-1864 earthquakes occurred up to four times a month, climaxing with a very severe earthquake on October 8, 1865, later called the "Great Quake," a name that would last until 1906. Walls waved and cracked, windows broke, plaster came down in showers, chimneys collapsed, bells rang and church steeples fell, and "general consternation ensued."[2] Santa Clara College suffered considerable damage as did most brick structures in town. Aftershocks persisted over the next several months, continuing to cause damage. These quakes, along with two consecutive years of torrential rains in 1864 and 1865, contributed to the loss of the once prolific adobe structures. When the first official survey of the Town was made in 1866, only 6 percent (17) of the 289 residences listed were made of adobe.

Although at a percentage rate less than that of the 1850s, the population continued to grow. The 1866 J.J. Bowen Survey of the town listed 231 property owners. By the general election of November 3, 1868, there were 765 registered voters in the Santa Clara Election District qualified to vote in the Santa Clara Precinct.[3] Along with those coming from other parts of the United States, various waves of immigrants from Europe and Asia continued to arrive in Santa Clara. Unrest in the German states toward the middle of the 1800s led to a large migration of Germanic peoples to the United States and starting in the 1850s many of these immigrants settled in Santa Clara. As their number rose dramatically during the 1860s through the 1880s they became very influential. Included among these German settlers were Frederick Christian Franck, Jacob Eberhard and Abram Block, men who made significant contributions to Santa Clara's political and economic development.

After his arrival in Santa Clara in 1855, F.C. Franck invested wisely, acquiring substantial property holdings. In 1871 he was elected to the state legislature and then re-elected two years later for a second term. During 1894-95 he served as a State Senator, representing California's 30th District of which encompassed most of Santa Clara County.

While in Sacramento, Jacob Eberhard met Mary Glein, whose father, Philip, owned the Santa Clara Tannery. In 1864 Jacob and Mary were wed and moved to Santa Clara, where, in 1867, Eberhard bought the Tannery from his father-in-law. Like Franck, Eberhard was also involved socially and politically in Santa Clara's growth. He was a founding member of the Odd Fellows and the Santa Clara Verein and also served as a member of the Town Board of Trustees.

In 1874, Abram Block, after meeting with reverses in his mercantile business because of the depreciation of mining stocks, moved from San Francisco to

Santa Clara where he purchased the Gould Fruit Ranch, which was planted with many varieties of fruit, including some of the choicest varieties of pears. Four years later he established the A. Block Fruit Company, and within ten years became widely known as a pear culturist, ranking among the most prominent horticulturists in California.

No German community was complete without a brewery, and by the 1880s Santa Clara had two. The largest was that of George Lauck, located at the corner of Alviso and Benton Streets, where Fire Station No.1 exists today.

A few Chinese had appeared in the Santa Clara area after the Gold Rush, such as Sing Kee, a cook, laundryman and weather prognosticator employed by Dr.

Saxe in 1860. It wasn't until 1863-64 that the first group of Chinese immigrants arrived, entering Santa Clara Valley as workers on the construction of the San Francisco and San Jose Railroad. While most early Chinese immigrants were employed by the railroad and as land clearers or domestics, many soon found work as farm laborers, working harder for less money than comparable Caucasian help. Despite hostility expressed towards them,[4] the Chinese remained dominant in agricultural field work until the turn of the century, with men like Kimberlin and Block employing them as laborers.[5]

In Santa Clara, there was no Chinatown proper. Laundry service was the most prevalent business opportunity for the Chinese immigrants and by 1886 half the

SING KEE AND FAMILY

A well known Chinese laundryman, Sing Kee gained local fame for his weather predictions, which were made using a frog which he kept in his shop. Sing Kee and Santa Clara University's Father Ricard were friendly rivals. At times, Sing Kee's forecasts understandably differed from those of the Father, who had developed a forecasting method using sunspots.

block on Franklin Street between Jackson and Main Streets was occupied by Chinese "wash houses." The businesses were located on the ground floor with living space above. In 1894 these Chinese laundries inspired Robert B. Roll and his partner William H. Werner to establish the Enterprise Laundry, the second laundry in Santa Clara County.[6]

The Town celebrated the nation's centennial on July 4, 1876 with a "Grand Procession," "Exercises at the Grove" (Cook's Grove), and "a grand display of Fireworks." Along with the program for the celebration, the centennial supplement to the *Santa Clara Echo* was filled with advertisements placed by the wide variety of businesses now established in the Town.

One year shy of being a quarter of a century old, Santa Clara's "downtown" now had a multitude of establishments, including dry goods stores, restaurants, harness shops, drug stores, saloons, ice cream and confection shops, hardware and furniture stores, hotels and lodging houses, bakeries, jewelers, real estate agents, the Bank of Santa Clara County and a bowling alley. In short, as one writer noted, "all the conveniences of a modern town."[7]

The growth of the Town and the construction of more substantial buildings necessitated a corresponding growth in the development of adequate fire protection. By 1871, with only one company, Columbian Engine No.1, the need for additional fire-fighting resources had become apparent, and Hook and Ladder Co. No.1 was organized. This was followed by the establishment of Mission Hose Co. in 1877, Tanner Hose Company in 1878, and Babcock Hose Brigade in 1879. In 1880, following the disbandment of Columbia Hose No.1, Hope Hose was organized. In 1891, after years of discussion, the first Town Hall – the city jail adjoining it – was constructed at the corner of Main and Benton Streets. The Town's fire bell was placed atop a wooden tower behind

CIVIC CROSSROADS

This view looking eastward down Franklin Street in 1874 shows the John Widney Building in the left foreground with the Mariposa Store on the opposite corner, across the intersection with Main Street.

the building.

Agriculture continued to play a prominent role in the Santa Clara economy, but now other industries that would bring renown to the Town were evolving. Originally located on the corner of Jackson and Liberty (Homestead) Streets, the Enterprise Mill and Lumber Co. had been founded by William Fosgate. After its purchase in 1874 by James P. Pierce, a new site on Bellomy Street, between Alviso and Lafayette Streets was acquired and the was mill relocated.[8] In 1880, the mill's name was changed when the Pacific Manufacturing Company purchased its assets and was incorporated.[9] By 1890, it had expanded to include the manufacture of such specialty items as Cyclone windmills and coffins and had entered the planing mill business.[10] As time passed, the Pacific Manufacturing Company would become known as the largest manufacturer of wood products on the West Coast.

While James P. Pierce is mainly known for his business enterprise, the Pacific Manufacturing Company, he also founded the Bank of Santa Clara County, erecting the building which housed it on the corner of Main and

Franklin Streets. He also developed the Pierce Isabella grape on his acreage at "*New Park*"[11] and it became one of the most popular varieties of grapes grown in the Santa Clara Valley.[12]

In 1892, the Santa Clara Tannery was incorporated as the Eberhard Tanning Company, and was now paying $50,000 a year in wages, providing a welcome stimulus to the Town's stability. Within the decade the tannery not only gained renown throughout the United States for its fine leather products but it also received worldwide prominence by providing leather goods to such places as the Royal House of Great Britain.

Another form of agricultural venture began in the last half of the 1870s with the establishment of seed farms, in particular those of two men, James M. Kimberlin and Charles Copeland Morse. After retiring in 1875, Kimberlin, a professor at the College of the Pacific since his arrival in 1852, devoted himself to agriculture, specializing in growing garden seeds. Starting with 199 acres, by 1904, J.M. Kimberlin & Co. would cultivate 1,000 acres in garden seeds, including onions, lettuce, beets, carrots, celery, radish, sweet peas, etc. The company was recognized as the largest garden seed growers on the Pacific Coast.

C.C. Morse, frequently referred to as the "American Seed King," and A.L. Kellogg in 1877 purchased the seed company which O.W. Wilson had started on 50 acres of land where Santa Clara High School is now located. When Kellogg retired in 1888 C.C. Morse became the sole owner. By then, 1,400 acres of land had been leased from the Martin Murphy estate in Sunnyvale and, later, land in Gilroy was leased from Thomas Rea. In 1892, Morse had a magnificent Queen Anne residence constructed in Santa Clara by local builder Zibeon O. Field. Today, listed on the National Register of Historic Places, his home still stands at 981 Fremont Street.

With California in the middle of a recession in 1877, the construction of the South Pacific Coast Railroad (a narrow gauge railroad) challenged the dominance of the Southern Pacific Railroad Company and proved to be a boost to the local economy. Cary Peebles sold to the narrow gauge railroad a portion of his farm and together with lands deeded by Abram Agnew, a tract was reserved for a depot which opened in 1878.[13] The location of this depot in the midst of the strawberry fields on the Santa Clara-Alviso Road resulted in the growth of the area north of the town. In 1888, the State constructed the California Hospital for the chronically insane (later called Agnews Insane Asylum) just east of the depot, and, by 1890, a post office had been established at "Agnew's Station" and a community (today called Agnews) laid out adjacent to the South Pacific Coast Railroad's station. In fact, for a while in the early 1890s, Agnews was actually two little villages, Agnew's Station and Bethlehem, with two post offices serving the community.[14]

In 1877, to handle the Town's increasing shipping needs, the original passenger depot was relocated to the western side of the tracks and joined to an existing freight house that abutted the Southern Pacific Railroad line. At the same time the freight house was enlarged. The following year, because of Cary Peebles influence, an S.P.C.RR depot was located in Santa Clara near the junction of Sherman and Benton Streets,[15] placing Santa Clara in the enviable position of having the two competing railroad lines within a couple blocks of each other. Santa Clara was now connected by rail not only to San Francisco and Monterey, but also to Alameda in the East Bay and west to Santa Cruz, including the small communities with their lumber resources in the midst of the Santa Cruz Mountains.

Improvements to the trolley system between Santa Clara and San Jose occurred in 1888, when electric trolleys

THE OTHER DEPOT

Located near the corner of Sherman and Benton Streets, Santa Clara's South Pacific Coast depot was larger than those in other towns, suggesting that the narrow gauge railroad considered Santa Clara "the little big time in its south bay operations."[18] Both the Town Board and landholders guaranteed the S.P.C.R.R. a franchise and the property for a substantial town depot.

began replacing horse cars on The Alameda. With the horses went the willows as the southernmost row of trees was cut down to make room for the electric trolley line.

In 1896, two years after starting the construction of its own water works, the Town constructed new municipal gas works buildings adjacent to the water works followed by the installation of the electric plant at the end of the year. This complex, called the Santa Clara Municipal Plant, was located on a parcel of land close to the railroad tracks where today the City of Santa Clara police department is located.[16]

As the nineteenth century neared its end, ethnic groups continued to immigrate to Santa Clara, contributing their cultural traditions to the town's development. During the late 1890s, Portuguese immigrants began to appear as a result of the King of Hawaii's arrangements to contract and transport families from Madeira and the Azores islands to work on the sugarcane and pineapple plantations in Hawaii. After discovering the harsh conditions of plantation life, many Portuguese immigrants moved on to California, settling in Santa Clara, where the climate was similar to their home. With their numbers increasing rapidly, in 1896 the Portuguese immigrants in Santa Clara dedicated Santa Clara's SES *(Sociedade Do Espírito Santo)* Hall, which served as a center for the observance of their traditional activities.

On the eve of the twentieth century, Santa Clara was almost 50 years old, with very little remaining of its mission days. It had a diverse population of 3,650 and the Town limits now expanded to cover three square miles, triple the extent at incorporation.[17] The community's needs for schools, churches, homes and transportation had been addressed. Its businesses were booming, and acres of developed agricultural land extended for miles in every direction.

GROWING YEARS

*In the early 1870s, the
Plat of Santa Clara
was compiled from the
1866 survey. It showed
not only the property
owners but also the
orchards and vineyards
that had developed in
the town in its
first two decades
of existence.*

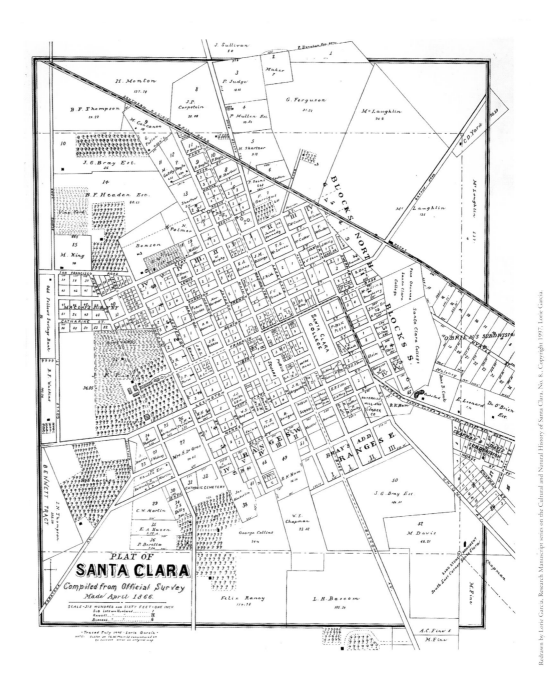

Redrawn by Lorie Garcia. Research Manuscript series on the Cultural and Natural History of Santa Clara. No. 8.. Copyright 1997, Lorie Garcia.

THE HARRIS-LASS PROPERTY

Johanna (Lass) Haynes and Betty Stevens

*Shown as Lot 23 on the plat map, within two years after its pur-
chase in 1864 Henry Harris had constructed a house and barn
and established an orchard on his property. The house and part
of the barn appear in this 1906 photograph, along with
Carolina, Johanna and Julia Lass, the granddaughters of
Captain Lass, who had purchased the property in June of that
year, and their aunt, Bertha Knauth.*

SANTA CLARA PANORAMA

This photo was taken in 1868 from the top of one of the University of the Pacific buildings, looking across the town

towards Santa Clara College. Lexington Street is on the right with University Avenue running across the center. The

Methodist church, its steeple lost in an earthquake that year, appears in the left skyline. Shown in the center skyline are

the Santa Clara College auditorium and Mission church.

Sourisseau Academy, San Jose State University

Santa Clara Historic Archives

*Frederick Christian Franck, looking
very young, and Caroline Durmeyer
are shown in this portrait made
shortly after their marriage in Santa
Clara on September 23, 1857.*

Santa Clara Historic Archives

HOME SWEET HOME

*F.C. and Caroline Franck constructed their home (a Queen Anne style mansion designed by
prominent architect Theodore Lenzen) on the northeast corner of Washington and Benton
Streets. Today the location is the site of a Wells Fargo bank.*

"LAYING OUT" IN THE FRANCK PARLOR

As was typical of the time, when Frederick Christian Franck died on December 29, 1902 at the age of 74, his funeral services were held at the family residence.

ALL IN ONE BUILDING

Located on the north side of Franklin Street, between Main and Washington Streets, the Franck Building housed the Santa Clara Library upstairs, with Regnart Meats and Menzel Hardware on the first floor.

THE FRANCK SADDLERY

After his arrival in Santa Clara in 1855, Frederick Christian Franck gained employment in Henry Messing's harness and saddle business. He soon became a partner and when Messing retired in 1859, F.C. continued the business under his name until 1875.

JACOB EBERHARD

Although only 27 years old when he arrived in Santa Clara in 1864, Jacob Eberhard already had considerable experience in the harness and saddle making business. Born in 1837 in Baden Germany, he was 15 when his family immigrated to Galena, Illinois, where Jacob learned this trade. He continued his involvement in the business when he came to California in 1858, where, after four years in the gold fields, he opened a harness shop in Sacramento.

MARY GLEIN EBERHARD

Mary Glein had emigrated with her parents from Cassel, Germany. Her father, Philip Glein, owned the Santa Clara Tannery that he had purchased in 1858 from John Henry Messing, who had married Mary's sister Louisa. Mary met Jacob in Sacramento, and on November 1, 1864, they were wed and moved to Santa Clara. Three years later he bought the tannery from his father-in-law.

THE EBERHARD HOUSE

In the mid 1870s, Jacob and Mary built a large Italianate home at 575 Grant Street, about a block from the tannery and along the main road connecting Santa Clara and San Jose. As the tannery prospered, the Eberhards made improvements to their home including the installation of indoor plumbing and electricity, which were major innovations in those days. Here they entertained friends and tannery employees at parties which gained wide renown.

William A. Wulf Historical Collection, Los Gatos Historian

A MODEL TANNERY

Having begun on a small scale, under Jacob's ownership the tannery grew until by the 1890s it produced 29,000 cow, 3000 calf and 100,000 sheep hides per year. By 1915 the Eberhard Tanning Company occupied 11 acres and was one of the largest tanneries in the world. Shown in the lithograph are the towering 80-foot-high smokestack which would fall in the 1906 earthquake, the office, which was housed in the original Mission adobe structure, and Tanner Hose Company, the volunteer fire company Jacob established in 1878.

Lorie Garcia Historical Collection

OPERATED BY A MODEL MAN IN A MODEL MANNER

The tannery provided employment for as many as one in four Santa Clarans at it's peak, including newly arrived immigrants from Germany, and provided a nice stimulus to the town's stability. As early as 1892, when it was incorporated as the Eberhard Tanning Company, the business had a yearly payroll of $50,000. According to his great grandson, Wayne Eberhard, Jacob "always paid his staff in silver and gold as (he) never seemed to trust the paper money of the day."

The A. Block Fruit Co.
FRUIT GROWERS & SHIPPERS
CALIFORNIA DECIDUOUS FRUITS

—CODES,—
ECONOMY
MODERN ECONOMY
REVISED ECONOMY
A.B.C. 4TH. & 5TH. EDITIONS

BLOCK'S

VIEW OF PEAR ORCHARD
VIEW OF PACKING HOUSE

Santa Clara, Cal., Sept 8th 09.

Wilcox Fruit Co,

By	3327#	Gros Prune	25—	41	58
	105	boxes B. Clairgeaus	75¢	78	75
	397	" B. Hardy	"	297	75
	18	" Duchesse	"	13	50
				431	58
To	315#	Gros for weight back		3	93
		check to balance		$427	6

A PLEASURE TO PAY

By the turn of the 20th century, both Abram Block's packing house and pear orchard covered extensive acreage, as illustrated in the company's letterhead. Besides the fruit grown on Block's orchards, hundreds of tons of fruit were bought from ranchers all over Santa Clara County.

THE PACKING WAREHOUSE

The packing warehouse structures for Abram Block's Fruit Company were located on the northeast corner of San Francisco Road and Scott's Lane (now El Camino Real and Scott Boulevard; the Bank of Santa Clara occupies part of the site). Shown in the photograph, the Fruit Company's high racked blue wagons with red running gear could be seen transporting boxes of packed pears to the South Pacific Coast Railroad warehouse at Sherman and Benton Streets as late as the 1920s.

PICKING PEARS

By 1907, Abram Block had nearly 200 acres of plum, pear and cherry orchards and had become one of the largest and best known shippers of green fruit on the west coast. Today, Mervyns' Plaza on the El Camino and Scott Boulevard, and the adjacent residential neighborhood are located on the pear orchard acreage shown in this photograph.

PACKING CHERRIES

The fruit packing season at the Block Fruit Packing Company began when the cherries ripened in May and continued until October, when the last of the winter pears were packed. Yearly, the considerable amount of fruit shipped from the A. Block Fruit Company to the eastern market gave employment to a large force of workers. While field work and picking fruit was done by men, fruit packing provided employment to women. The income of many Santa Clara families was augmented by these jobs, including a large number of grammar school and high school youngsters who were sure of summer jobs.

A WELL-AGED BEER

> Born in Germany in 1838, George Lauck came to America when he was 16 and, like
> Jacob Eberhard, settled in Galena, Illinois. There, Lauck learned the art of brewing. After
> serving in the Civil War, Lauck came to San Francisco in 1868 and then moved to
> Castroville. In 1878 he settled in Santa Clara, where he purchased the Santa Clara
> Brewery, located on the northeast corner of Benton and Alviso Streets. Equipped with the
> latest machinery and brewing kettles that had an enormous storage capacity that enabled
> the delivery of well-aged beer at all times, the Santa Clara Brewery gained an outstanding
> reputation throughout the county. Shown in the photograph taken on October 6, 1893
> are (Left to Right), Chas. Koenig, an unidentified man, Frank P. Lauck, Gus Ritter, Fred
> Fischer and Jacob Lauck.

Leonard McKay's Clyde Arbuckle Collection

THE HAND WASHING ROOM

First located on the second floor of Edwin Davies' machine shop at the corner of Liberty (Homestead) and Jackson Streets, the Enterprise Laundry burned to the ground eight months later. The business was then relocated to an old distillery building at 867 Sherman Street, which was leased and remodeled for laundry purposes. A large trade was established in Santa Clara and neighboring cities and an average of 25 people were employed, with horse-drawn wagons picking up and delivering the laundry. Besides the laundering of clothes, another service, somewhat akin to it, was provided by this business when Robert Roll installed three wood-framed zinc bathtubs in one corner where a man could take a bath for a quarter.

Santa Clara Historic Archives

ROBERT B. ROLL

Shown (right) with Fred Fischer (left), Robert B. Roll arrived in Santa Clara in 1878 and went to work for the Santa Clara Tannery, remaining there for 16 years. In 1894, in partnership with William H. Werner, he established the Enterprise Steam Laundry. Along with activities related to his business, Robert B. Roll gave time to the community. He served on the town's Board of Trustees, the Board of School Trustees and helped organize the Santa Clara Commercial League, becoming its first president.

Santa Clara Historic Archives

A NEW NAME

For most of the 76 years it was in operation the Enterprise Laundry was managed by members of the Roll family. However, it was renamed the Sainte Claire Laundry, Inc., during the two and one-half years it was owned by Everett Strickland. In 1970, the Sainte Claire Laundry closed its doors and the land was sold to Santa Clara University for expansion purposes.

A CENTENNIAL SPECIAL

From the time of its incorporation, Santa Clara celebrated the Fourth of July. One of the grandest celebrations occurred in 1876 with the centennial celebration of the nation's independence. A four-page special issue of the Santa Clara newspaper, The Santa Clara Echo, carried not only the program for the festivities, but also advertisements of most of the businesses which had by then been established in the town.

HOPE HOSE

Prior to marching in a parade, members of Hope Hose pose in front of their building located at 920 Washington Street, between Franklin and Liberty (Homestead) Streets.

TO PRESERVE AND PROTECT

In 1878 Tanner Hose Company was formed by the employees of the Santa Clara Tannery and Jacob Eberhard purchased a hose cart and 500 feet of hose for it. It was originally intended to provide protection for the tannery. By 1888, when a building to house the company was constructed, Tanner Hose had become one of the five volunteer companies that provided fire protection to the town.

FIRST TOWN HALL

Constructed in 1891, the first Town Hall was located at the corner of Main and Benton Streets, with the jail housed at the rear of the building.

LOOKING NORTH

The City Hall and jail, with the wooden bell tower used to sound fire alarms behind it, appears on the far left side in this photograph taken from the Methodist Church steeple, looking north down Main Street from Liberty (Homestead) Street, across Franklin and Benton Streets. (Note the trolley on Franklin Street crossing Main.)

"NEW PARK"

In 1895, shortly before he died, James P. Pierce sold "New Park" along with 34 acres to Judge Hiram G. Bond for $25,000. While Judge Bond owned it, writer Jack London, a friend of the judge's sons, was a frequent visitor and is believed to have used "New Park" in his novel, The Call of the Wild, *as the starting locale, which he described as,* "It stood back from the road half hidden among the trees through which glimpses could be caught of the wide cool veranda" *and* "The House was approached by graveled driveways which wound about through wide spreading lawns and under interlacing boughs of tall poplars." *Today, the Carmelite Monastery (built in 1916) occupies the site of the house, although the tank house and carriage house remain. Wilson School and residential development cover much of the orchard and vineyard land.*

History of Santa Clara County by Eugene Sawyer, 1922

JAMES PIERONNET PIERCE

Born in Pennsylvania, the enterprising James P. Pierce came to California in 1854, where during the following two decades he made a fortune in hydraulic mining operations in Yuba County (at one time owning the famed Empire Mine in Grass Valley) and pioneered the sugar and white pine industry. In 1866 he purchased his estate "New Park" in Santa Clara and in 1874, the Enterprise Mill and Lumber Company. This company became the Pacific Manufacturing Company.

Lorie Garcia Historical Collection

AT HOME

This interior view of "New Park" shows the ornate furnishings with which the rooms were decorated.

Santa Clara Historic Archives

EVERY PRODUCT MADE OF WOOD

During the 81 years following its incorporation as the Pacific Manufacturing Company, thousands were employed at the PM Co. plant in Santa Clara. Products ranging from coffins to cyclone windmills were among the specialty items made by the mill in its early days. Later it manufactured virtually every product made of wood. The 1904 publication, "Progressive Santa Clara" describes the Company as "operating one of the largest and best equipped manufacturing plants devoted to this branch of trade in the state," further stating that "employment is given to about 300 men in the manufacture of all kinds of mill work, sash, doors…molding, stair work…bank and office fixtures, all kinds of church work, including pulpits, pews etc." Today, part of the site is occupied by Santa Clara University and the rest lies under the beginning section of the El Camino re-route (Highway 82).

IMPRESSIVE ADVERTISING

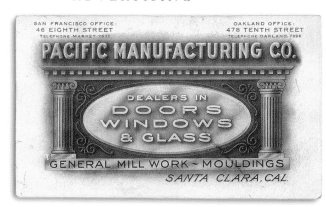

William A. Wulf Historical Collection, Los Gatos Historian

By 1905, branch offices had been opened in San Francisco and Oakland.

TRANSPORTATION UPGRADE

When the passenger depot was relocated across the tracks in 1877, it was attached to an existing 30' x 60' freight house that had been constructed several years earlier. At that time, because of the volume of agricultural products that were being shipped from Santa Clara, the freight house was increased to its present size of 32' x 160'. The following year, in conjunction with the construction of the South Pacific Coast depot, the loading dock was put in. As shown in this 1904 photo, it was approximately 100' longer than it exists today.

RAILROAD CROSSING

Between 1887 and 1893, after Southern Pacific had acquired the South Pacific Coast RR in 1886, the crossing, which had been 1800 feet north of the Santa Clara Depot, was relocated. Looking north, this picture shows the new (second) crossing approximately 700 ft. south of the depot with a southbound passenger train approaching it. The narrow gauge tracks are to the right (east) of the main track. The depot appears in the center background with the town's water tanks dominating the horizon in the left background. Over the years there were spectacular wrecks at this crossing, most due to human error.

CHARLES COPELAND MORSE

Charles Copeland Morse worked for 12 years as a house painting contractor following his arrival in California but in 1877 he purchased the Pacific Seed Gardens and soon became known as the "American Seed King."

MARIA (LANGFORD) MORSE

Maria Langford married Charles Copeland Morse and they and their four children lived in a residence on the grounds of the Pacific Seed Co., located on San Francisco Road, a half mile west of Santa Clara, before the construction of their mansion on Fremont Street.

GROWN FROM SEED

Located on the San Francisco Road, west of Santa Clara, was the main warehouse of the C.C. Morse & Company. With hundreds of acres planted with flowers and vegetables, at harvest time 500 men were employed in gathering crops from thousands of different beds and fields. Planting and harvesting were carried on year round, with sowing timed so no seeds were harvested during the rainy season.

AN IDEAL HOME

Shortly after its construction of C.C. Morse's mansion, an article in the May 15, 1892 San Jose Daily

Mercury described it as "the largest and most striking example of modern architecture in Santa Clara. The

grounds occupied by this handsome residence cover an entire block in the heart of the town." The article fur-

ther states that "at the rear of the house are the extensive stables and carriage room, the most commodious and

the handsomest in Santa Clara." This magnificent Queen Anne mansion and the carriage house still exist at

the northeast corner of Fremont and Washington Streets.

JOHN JOSEPH MONTGOMERY

John Joseph Montgomery is shown standing with his ash wood tandem-wing glider "Santa Clara" in the Santa Clara College vineyard prior to the historic flight of April 29, 1905.

JOHN JOSEPH MONTGOMERY "FATHER OF BASIC FLIGHT"

When the history of manned flight is discussed, the accomplishments of the Wright brothers at Kitty Hawk, North Carolina, in and around 1900, are usually the main topic of conversation. But there is a definite Santa Clara connection to man's attempts to fly and that connection is John Joseph Montgomery, the first American to build a controllable glider that actually flew.

Montgomery, who was born in Yuba City, California in 1858, was fascinated by birds in flight at an early age. By the time he was 11 and living in Oakland he began experimenting with kites and other flying apparatus and he dreamed of the day man would be able to build an aircraft that would allow him to fly.

Completing his secondary education at St. Joseph's Academy in Oakland, Montgomery enrolled at Santa Clara College in 1874. He subsequently transferred to St. Ignatius College in San Francisco, where he received a B.S. degree in 1879 and a M.S. degree in science the following year. By 1882 he was continuing his experiments with flight on the family ranch near San Diego.

Shortly after eight a.m. on an August morning in 1883, from the rim of a windy mesa in Otay near San Diego, Montgomery made man's first controlled flight in a heavier-than-air craft, when he soared some 600 feet in a stable controlled flight.[1] This achievement which "preceded by some 10 years the famous glider flights of Otto Lilienthal and by 20 years the historic powered flights of the Wright brothers,"[2] led to a momentous flight in Santa Clara 22 years later.

For the next ten years, Montgomery continued to research and experiment, concluding that the parabolic airfoil shape with its "low-pressure area" was the most efficient wing design, a principle that would not be recognized by many until 1910. In 1893, Montgomery presented his first public paper, "Soaring Flight," to the Conference on Aerial Navigation at the Columbian Exhibition in Chicago, in which he described his concepts of wing-spread-ratios and wing curvature, both based on his study of birds. Sponsored and encouraged to do this by his friend Octave Chanute, he could not know that later Chanute would pass on the information he gained from Montgomery to the Wright brothers, cautioning them to be silent about the source.

While a student at Santa Clara College Montgomery had formed a close friendship with Rev. Robert E. Kenna, S.J. and this friendship brought him back to Santa Clara in 1897, where he accepted a teaching post at the college as a professor of Engineering. Here he continued his experiments with flying, working on a series of model gliders that eventually would lead to one he named the *Santa Clara*. On April 29, 1905, he conducted man's first flight that ended in a controlled landing at a pre-designated site. Victor Lougheed (later "Lockheed") described Montgomery as "The Father of Basic Flight" and Alexander Graham Bell stated that "All subsequent attempts in aviation must begin with the Montgomery machine."

Some 15,000 people watched as Frank Hamilton's large hot-air balloon lifted Montgomery's aeroplane-glider, the *Santa Clara*, piloted by Daniel John Maloney, from the college vineyard (a granite shaft on the University campus marks the site). Cutting loose at 4000 feet, Maloney maneuvered the aircraft for 20 minutes at speeds of up to eight miles an hour, executing every possible movement before safely landing at the cho-

sen site (the southeast corner of Alviso and Poplar Streets). This was the first public high-air flight of man with official witnesses, newspaper observers and photographers.[3] Detailed accounts appeared simultaneously on April 30, 1905 in such papers as the San Francisco Examiner, the Los Angeles Times, the San Francisco Call, the San Francisco Bulletin, the San Jose Mercury-Herald, the Philadelphia Public Ledger, the New York Times, the Baltimore Sun and the Oakland Times.

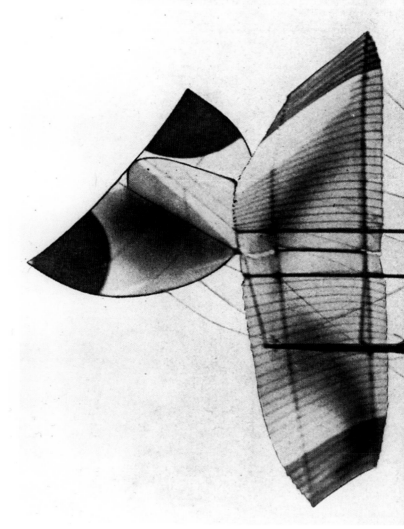

C. 1904, Santa Clara University Archives

DANIEL JOHN MALONEY

Clad in his eye-catching red tights, Daniel J. Maloney, aged 26, maneuvers the "Santa Clara" as shown in this May 21, 1905, San Francisco Call photo.

A flight held at the San Jose Agricultural Park on May 21 did not go as smoothly as the one on April 29. The *Santa Clara* was jerked loose at 150 feet and a second attempt had to be made in a sister ship named the *California*. On this try, Maloney unsuccessfully struggled to release the craft from the hot-air balloon and was forced to ride the hot-air balloon down almost to Gilroy, 30 miles away.

A last flight, on July 18, 1905, resulted in Maloney's death. The League of the Cross Cadets, encamped at Santa Clara College, had asked Montgomery for a demonstration flight of his aircraft with Maloney at the controls. The balloon with the plane ascended to about 4,000 feet, when Maloney cut the plane loose and after an easy drop straightened out for a glide. What Maloney could not see was that the dangling balloon release cables had caught in the "control tower" above his head. It was only after he had cut loose that he felt the snag of the rope and although struggling desperately, he could not control the damaged plane and started his fatal plunge. The descent started a little south of the campus with the dive in an easterly direction toward the Eberhard Tannery. Roy

Graves, a member of the League, later said, "It was the opinion of those that were watching him at the tannery that he was trying to land in the tanbark pile which would have helped to break his fall, but that he fell to the ground instead."[4]

The tragedy devastated Montgomery. This, combined with the destruction of his workshop and remaining gliders the next year by the earthquake on April 18, resulted in his pursuit of non-aeronautical activities for several years. He focused on teaching and inventing electrical devices, although he did continue to work on a significant discovery he had made—how to obtain maximum lift and stability from a cambered wing surface. Early in 1910, Montgomery announced his plans for a monoplane and his marriage to Regina Cleary on June 30, 1910, provided the incentive for perfecting it. The newlyweds moved into a house in Santa Clara, at 1199 Market Street (on the northeast corner of Jackson and Market Streets). With the love and encouragement of his wife, Montgomery succeeded in his plan to add an engine to his plane, which would guarantee power lift and distance flying. In 1911, he had rails laid down from the crest of a hill in Evergreen Valley, just south of San Jose, and in a two week period that October, Montgomery made 55 successful flights from this launching site, at the control of his monoplane *The Evergreen*.[5] Then on October 31, tragedy struck Montgomery for the final time. While airborne between 13 and 23 feet, the craft stalled, side slipped, fell gently, striking the right wingtip on the ground, and overturned. His head was pierced by one of the overlong stove bolts used to hold the main wing supports to the fuselage, and within two hours John Joseph Montgomery, the first person to successfully fly a heavier-than-air man-carrying aircraft, was dead, but his significant contributions to flying will live forever.[6]

Clyde Arbuckle Collection

" ... WHERE HEALTH
AND PLENTY ARE
THE PORTIONS OF
HER PEOPLE. "

S anta Clara began the 20th century on a festive note. Santa Clara College
was observing its golden anniversary and celebrated the occasion in high
style. In addition to four days of special events on the campus surrounding graduation, there was a two day civic celebration in March complete with
banquets and a parade replete with marching units and horse-drawn floats.[1] More
than the prestige brought by the college, the Town had other reasons to feel good
about itself. Its population was growing as more people were attracted to the
healthful climate and increasing opportunities to be found in what would soon
be called the Valley of Heart's Delight. Some 3,600 residents of the township had
increased within the first decade of the century to around 5,000. Agricultural
production continued to expand and manufacturing enterprises began to grow.
The first families of the Town spearheaded the development of an increasingly
middle class culture. Public services became more extensive and sophisticated.
Finally, in the first third of the new century, Santa Clara began to separate itself
from its larger neighbor, San Jose, with a myriad of social and cultural organizations, recreational and educational facilities.

In an attempt to encourage the town's residential and commercial growth, the forerunner of today's Chamber of Commerce, the Santa Clara Commercial League, printed a number of pamphlets early in the new century. Perhaps the League had a dual meaning in mind when it described Santa Clara as progressive at the beginning of the national progressive movement.

Lorie Garcia Historic Collection

In 1902 the Santa Clara Commercial League, later the Santa Clara Chamber of Commerce, was formed to promote the City and attract new residents and businesses. In a series of informational booklets, the Commercial League emphasized the Town's progressive attitudes and described it as "an abode where fruit and flowers lend enchantment to the eye, and where health and plenty are the portions of her people."[2] It was an active advocate for bringing new families and businesses to town and supported with funding a variety of civic improvements including the paving of sidewalks and the installation of street lights on Franklin Street.

One of the Commercial League's major accomplishments was attracting the Pratt-Low Preserving Company to open a cannery just south of the Southern Pacific Railroad depot. By 1922, it sprawled over ten acres and employed between 400 and 1000 people during the harvesting season. Cherries, peaches, pears, plums, grapes and tomatoes were processed and shipped not only throughout the country but the entire world as well.

In addition to processing plants, established fruit packing companies expanded their operations in the first third of the century. By 1907 the A. Block Fruit Packing Company had some 200 acres of plum and peach trees which it picked and, supplemented by fruit from other farms, took to its packing sheds, packed, and, sent by rail to eastern markets and later around the world. After Rosenberg Bros. opened a branch in Santa Clara in 1915, it claimed to be the largest fruit packer in California with eight branches around the state. Years later, the novelist Wallace Stegner commented: "The dried peach pies that my mother baked in Saskatchewan during World War I almost certainly came from here… This was a *par excellence* fruit bowl, and it spread its fragrant bounty world-wide.[3]

Commercial and industrial enterprises grew side by side with an expanding agricultural sector. Some businesses, like the Eberhard Tannery, continued their activities. Others continued under a variety of names. The Universal Bakery opened in 1891 on Franklin Street. Over the years as it changed owners it became the Voltmer Bakery, the Smith Bakery and the Jewel Bakery until it was purchased by William Wilson in 1921 and renamed Wilson's Jewel Bakery. Eighty years later it continues under that name. The Pacific Manufacturing Company, with its origins in 19th century Santa Clara, had established a number of branches in the bay area by the beginning of the 20th century. The great earthquake of 1906 caused it to consolidate its operations and its mill ran 16 hours a day to supply the building materials necessary to help reconstruct the devastated area. During World War I, the company began manufacturing airplane parts and by the late 1920s built a new mill and main office on The Alameda across from the University to accommodate its growing business. The attraction of new companies and the expansion of existing ones, together with the booming agricultural sector, reflected Santa Clara's increasingly mixed economy.

One of the characteristics of turn-of-the-century America was a nationwide movement to improve the lives of its citizens, especially those who lived in cities and larger towns. One of the leaders of this Progressive movement, Frederic C. Howe, once noted that the challenge to cities was to provide "decent human existence" to its residents.[4] Santa Clara recognized this responsibility as it improved its water supply and developed the delivery of electricity through publicly owned utilities.

Following a fire in 1894 that dramatically demonstrated the town's low level of water pressure, the electorate voted to establish its own Town water system rather than rely on the San Jose Water Company or private wells. The bond issues provided for the purchase of two Worthington pumps, capable of pumping 50,000 gallons of water per hour. Four elevated redwood tanks, each holding 45,000 gallons of water, were built and filled with water from four 225 foot-deep wells. Sixteen miles of pipe were laid, 53 hydrants were established and 400 house connections were made. In this way, not only did the Town better protect its residents against fire but it also brought running water to numerous households. But when the earthquake of 1906 destroyed the tanks, the Town was left with no water storage supply. To replace the fallen tanks, a cistern was constructed along with a 100,000 gallon elevated tank. Twenty years later, a civic improvement plan was funded by the voters to replace the old water mains, create some new ones, and install pipes to all city lots.

Meeting the Town's electrical needs would soon follow. Looking at the high cost of street lighting, the town trustees decided that establishing a locally controlled electrical service would be cheaper than and superior to that provided by a private company. A surprise surplus from the water bond issue would be used to construct a lighting plant. By December 1896, 46 street lights were up and running. After initially generating its own electricity, in 1904 the electric department contracted with the United Gas and Electric Company of San Jose for its current and became simply a distribution utility. Eighty years later, the City would again begin generating its own electricity.

Public safety departments, while remaining essentially unpaid volunteer groups, were also increasingly better equipped and more professionalized. The five volunteer fire companies of the 19th century, merged in the first decade of the 20th into a consolidated volunteer fire department. The Town was divided into four districts, with each of the hose companies having responsibility for the area in which they were located. In 1913 the Town purchased its first motor-driven fire engine. A Ford Model-T hook and ladder was purchased in 1924 and three years later, a motor driven pumper was added. The pumper continued in service until after World War II. While a friendly rivalry existed among the volunteers based on their individual historic companies, frequent social activities such as barbecues and card parties served to bring about a sense of community and common purpose in their firefighting.

A formal police department did not lend itself to volunteers and was slower in coming. But the new century created new challenges calling for new solutions. The frontier character of the Town was gone. Grain and cattle-raising had given way to fruit growing and its attendant industry. One of the major challenges was the automobile, which added traffic safety to the marshal's list of responsibilities. Marshal "Pete" Fallon, who served Santa Clara from 1911 to 1946, bought his own motorcycle to help enforce new traffic laws. A full time traffic officer was hired in 1924 but he was also given the additional duty of serving as meat inspector. The following year another traffic officer was hired. (Of course they were expected to provide their own motorcycles.) Crimefighting did not seem to be either a major problem or a high priority.

Alexis de Tocqueville, the astute French observer of American society in the early 19th century, noted that the United States was a nation of joiners.[5] That certainly seems to be true of 20th century Santa Clarans. To the existing social and fraternal orders like the Odd Fellows, Masons and Eastern Star, were added new groups. The Native Sons of the Golden West organized a parlor in 1902. The Order of Red Men and its women's counterpart, the Order of Pocahontas, established a "tribe" to

keep alive the customs of a "vanishing race." The annual *Festa* and parade sponsored by the Portuguese immigrants' Society of the Holy Spirit (SES) attracted tens of thousands of participants and spectators.[6]

FESTA TIME

The influence of Portuguese settlers in the town of Santa Clara and the Bay Area has been significant. Attracted first by the Gold Rush and then in the latter part of the 19th century by the fertile land of the valley, immigrants from Portugal proper, from the Azores and often via Hawaii moved into the region. Settling in as farmers and dairymen, they maintained close-knit cultural ties through the establishment of a fraternal organization, the Society of the Holy Spirit, in 1896. The SES Hall, shown in the picture, served as the gathering place for social functions. The annual parade and festival in honor of the Holy Spirit attracted large crowds. Note that the cow in the cart is bedecked with flowers on the way to the Festa

Among the groups founded in this period was the Santa Clara Woman's Club in 1904. By the end of that year this civic improvement club had 70 members, including wives and daughters of the town's most influential citizens. Through fund raisers and its members' own labor it undertook to clear the town plaza of weeds, plant shrubs, trees and flowers, and pay for a gardener. It urged improvements of the train depot and sponsored outdoor rallies in support of women's suffrage. In 1913, the Woman's Club bought the Peña Adobe for its meeting place. Originally part of Mission Santa Clara, it was built in the late 18th century. Still serving as headquarters for the Woman's Club, it is thought to be the oldest surviving adobe in Northern California.

One group that did not fare well during this period was the Santa Clara Verein, a German social organization. Aimed at maintaining German culture and customs, it claimed as members many of the Town's first citizens. Although thriving for almost 50 years, it began to decline at the outbreak of World War I because of significant anti-German feeling and the aging of its founding members. When Santa Clarans formed a "home guard" that trained with weapons and prepared to repel any possible German attack and demonstrated their patriotism by banning the teaching of German in the high school, its days were numbered.[7]

The need for additional educational and recreational facilities became increasingly apparent to the citizenry. While a school system of one grammar and one high school filled the educational needs of Santa Clara for years, the Board of Education in 1904 discussed the need to separate the high school from the grammar school since both were housed in the same building. The cornerstone for Santa Clara High School was laid in

1905 and it opened that fall with an enrollment of 175. Having outgrown its student body by 1921, a new, larger high school was built adjacent to the old one. The original brick building became the first intermediate school in Santa Clara. Meanwhile, the old grammar school got older. By 1912, the school trustees decided to replace it with a new school. Fremont School opened in 1913. There would not be another school built for 20 years.

Libraries and parks were expanded in this period to help strengthen both the minds and the bodies of Santa Clarans. A public Town Library was opened in 1903 with 800 volumes when the libraries of the old Library Association, the Women's Christian Temperance Union and the Santa Clara Book Club were combined. The Town assumed responsibility for the library when it moved into the second floor of the newly built City Hall in 1914. Developing out of the Mission's horse corral, the City Plaza Park until 1955 served as public open space for a variety of recreational and social activities. A bandstand was added about 1900 and the Woman's Club undertook its landscaping soon afterwards. In 1900 the city also purchased the land for its first municipal park, Lafayette Park, today called Marsalli, which has become a favorite softball venue.

While Santa Clara's population remained relatively constant between 1910 and 1930, its civic infrastructure matured. Symbolic of that development was the decision to amend the Town's 1872 charter. In 1927 a new charter changed the title of the President of the Board of Trustees to that of Mayor, increasing that office's powers to coordinate, direct and modernize the administrative departments. Even more symbolically, the new charter changed the name of the municipality from Town of Santa Clara to the City of Santa Clara.

CITY HALL SANTA CLARA CALIF

AN ALL-PURPOSE
BUILDING

A new Town (later City) Hall opened in 1913 on the corner of Franklin and Washington Streets.

A versatile structure, in addition to housing the town's administrative offices, the marshal's office

and town jail, its second floor was occupied by the public library which for the first time came

directly under the authority of the town's trustees.

SJ-100 LAWS

A KEEN EYE

Alice Hare (1859-1942) was one of the foremost commercial photographers in the Santa Clara Valley at the turn of the 20th century. She and her family settled in Santa Clara in 1895. Having raised four sons and working out of her home on Madison Street, Hare used for her subjects what she found around her. Thus she captured for posterity not only agricultural and natural subjects, but also a variety of historic sites and the last vestiges of moldering adobe buildings. Her photos appeared at the St. Louis Exposition in 1904, in commercial publications and in a number of self-published collections of her work. She moved to the Central Valley in 1911 and then to Berkeley in 1924. Having abandoned photography, in later life she became a librarian and short story writer. She died a pauper in 1924.

Leaders of the emerging genteel class in Santa Clara, Fred and Maud Shuld Franck reflect the comfortable domesticity characteristic of the early 20th century.

Elayne Franck, Bea Lichtenstein

Elayne Franck, Bea Lichtenstein

Brian Lichtenstein Photo

Designed by the prominent local architect Louis Lenzen, the home of Frederick Christian Franck II, scion of one of the town's earliest settlers, was built in 1905.

The next generation: the Franck children (from left), Delilah, Gladys and Frederick III accompanied by another sign of middle class home life — Buster the dog.

Warburton Family Collection

THE MISSION BANK
of SANTA CLARA
Commercial and Savings

—— DIRECTORS ——
ROBERT A. FATJO, President   H. L. WARBURTON, Cashier   JOHN LANINI
DAVID J. SPENCE, Vice President   ROBERT R. SYER, Attorney   LUIS G. FATJO, Asst. Cashier

Lorie Garcia Historical Collection

*Another son of one of the founding Anglo-
American settlers, Henry Luke Warburton played
a significant role in the growth of turn-of-the-
century Santa Clara. In addition to being
involved with his wife in a variety of civic
affairs, H.L. Warburton organized the Mission
Bank of Santa Clara in 1910 which served as a
lending agency for a wide spectrum of commercial endeavors in 'progressive' Santa Clara. In
later years he organized the Garden City Bank
and Trust and became manager of its Santa
Clara branch.*

A BUSY SUMMER DAY

Workers at the Rosenberg Bros. fruit cutting shed in the mid-1920s. After cutting, the fruit was placed to dry in the frames in the foreground of the picture. After the drying period, the fruit would be packaged and distributed nationally. Men, women and children worked side by side in this summertime enterprise.

Ron Rose Collection

THE PLACE

The Pratt-Low Preserving Company, located south of the Southern Pacific Railroad depot, opened its doors in Santa Clara in 1905. By 1922, its original three acre site had more than tripled in size in order to permit the processing and shipping of 10 million cans annually around the globe.

Ron Rose Collection

CUTTING ROOM

After the boxes of fruit had been unloaded in the receiving area and weighed, they were brought to the cutting room where they were cut, pitted or cored, and graded for size and quality.

WORLD FAMOUS

Colorful labels such as these made 'Santa Clara' household words for premium fruit. The labels described the contents of the can and also served as pictorial representations of the source of the fruit as seen through the eyes of the artist.

Bea Lichtenstein Collection

A TOWER OF STEEL

By the turn of the century, Santa Clara's water supply storage was
contained in these four tanks towering 80 feet above the ground on
a steel platform. Each tank could hold 45,000 gallons for a total
reserve supply of 180,000 gallons. The water was pumped from
wells 225 feet deep.

A RUDE AWAKENING

A dramatic result of the great earthquake that devastated San Francisco in 1906 was the destruction of the structure which held Santa Clara's water supply storage. With the storage tanks shattered, the Town was left without any water storage capability. Subsequently, the Town built a cistern in which to hold water and a 100,000 gallon elevated tank which combined held two million gallons of water. In 1932, another two million gallons of water storage capacity was added with the construction of two ground storage tanks.

SANTA CLARA GOTHIC

The oldest Protestant denomination in Santa Clara is Methodism. Beginning with worship service in an adobe church in the 1850s, a more permanent looking structure was soon erected. The foundation for the 'Brick Church' was laid in 1862 and the church was completed in 1867. Of Gothic design, with buttresses and pinnacles, it was capped by a steeple some 150 feet high. It was located on the present site of Liberty Towers at Homestead and Main Streets.

WHAT HATH GOD WROUGHT

A glorious Easter was celebrated in the Brick Church on April 15, 1906. Decorated with over 3,000 lilies, more than 600 worshipers were present for the last service. Three days later, the church was demolished by the 1906 earthquake. The following Sunday services were held in a tent. Within two years a new church was constructed on the site and remained there for almost 60 years until the Methodist Episcopal Church moved to its current Civic Center location.

PATRIOTIC SPIRIT

The Independence Day parade in 1917 marches on Franklin Street under the electric sign proclaiming 'Santa Clara.' Illuminated first in April 1916, the sign spanned 36 feet and weighed 900 pounds. The arch at Franklin and Washington Streets was a part of the continued promotion of the town as a progressive location for living and working.

Lorie Garcia Historic Collection

ALL THINGS MODERN

Santa Clara Historic Archives

To complement its newly consolidated volun-

teer fire department, the Town purchased its

first motor-driven fire engine from the

Seagraves Company in 1913. A chemical

wagon, it carried two 25-gallon tanks of

chemical extinguishers, 200 feet of one inch

rubber hose, and 1,000 feet of two inch hose.

NOT YOUR FATHER'S MODEL-T

Santa Clara Historic Archives

In the early 1920s, a second motor driven

fire engine was purchased, a Ford Model-T

hook and ladder, to continue the modern-

ization of fire-fighting techniques. It was

used to fight fires for some 20 years and

still looked good in this photo taken over

30 years later. Both the Seagraves engine

and the Model-T exist today as part of the

fire department's antique apparatus collection.

MARSHAL PETE FALLON

For almost a century, the responsibility of maintaining law and order in Santa Clara fell to the Town Marshal. One of the notable marshals was George Peter "Pete" Fallon. A native of Santa Clara, Fallon served as marshal from 1911 to 1946. Fallon was not only a one-man police force but also for a time tax collector, street superintendent and meat inspector. As automobiles became more common and before a traffic officer was hired in 1924, Fallon monitored traffic safety with his self-purchased Indian brand motorcycle. Known to all Santa Clarans of the times, he was a favorite of children for distributing candy and fruit from in front of his office at Christmas time.

KEEPER OF THE PEACE

Another native Santa Claran, James E. Glendenning, was born in 1855. Having attended the College of the Pacific, he was first elected Justice of the Peace in 1903. Although not a lawyer, he established a reputation for handling family and neighborhood disputes fairly and firmly. He served 18 years, continuing to be reelected until his sudden death in 1921.

BUSINESSLIKE SOCIABILITY

The oldest of the numerous fraternal organizations that sprang up in Santa Clara was the Independent Order of Odd Fellows. Although most of these groups were formed early in the 20th century and immediately after World War II, Santa Clara Lodge No. 52 of the IOOF was organized in 1856. The Odd Fellows Hall on Franklin and Washington Streets was built in 1868. With commercial enterprises on the first floor providing a source of income, the second story contained a large lodge room, anterooms and reception rooms. Renting out the hall to other associations without their own meeting places, produced additional income for the lodge. The building was leveled in 1965 as part of the downtown renewal project.

Silva / Kenyon Family Collection

Santa Clara Historic Archives

Harold Slavens delivered mail in Santa Clara for more than 40 years. When he began his rural route in 1903 he first used a bicycle and then a horse and buggy. By 1920 he brought mail to the outlying parts of the township by automobile. The last 20 years of his postal career were spent walking a city route.

A team of horses haul a double wagon load of 12 cords of wood along an unpaved Santa Clara street.

Santa Clara Historic Archives

Santa Clara Historic Archives

George Milovich, the greengrocer, selling his pro- duce from a horse-drawn wagon along the streets of Santa Clara.

The dirt streets of Santa Clara were transformed into 'modern' thorough- fares during the first third of the 20th century. After having done the down- town area along Franklin and Main Streets, the pavers turned to the residential areas - today's Old Quad.

Santa Clara Historic Archives

If the streets were paved, they had to be kept clean. The town's first street sweeper, Antone Pacheco, in the mid-1920s helping to keep Santa Clara beautiful.

RECLAIMING THE PAST

The formal opening of the Woman's Club house in 1914 was a gala affair. First meeting in the Odd Fellows Hall in 1904, then in a variety of locations, the Santa Clara Woman's Club obtained a permanent home when it purchased the Peña Adobe. Originally part of Mission Santa Clara, the building became the property of Don José Peña in 1840. Over the years, the Woman's Club has removed an interior wall and added a tile floor but remains committed to keeping it as close as possible to its original state.

A SPIRITUAL OASIS

The Carmelite Order is a Roman Catholic religious community of men and women dedicated to a life of prayer. Originally coming to San Francisco in 1908, the Carmelite nuns decided to establish its permanent monastery in Santa Clara in 1914. Their great benefactor was Alice Phelan Sullivan, whose daughter had entered the order in Boston. Through her brother, Senator James Phelan, and her son, Noel Sullivan, the Pierce-Bond estate, "New Park" was acquired as a location for the monastery. Construction for a permanent monastery began on the property at Lincoln and Benton Streets in 1916 and the chapel was completed in 1918. In the aerial view, c.1930, the monastery and its newly planted olive orchard is shown amid the remains of the estate gardens. Designed by the distinguished church architect, Charles D. Maginnis, the monastery combined the idea of the medieval monastery, the traditions of the Carmelite Order of Renaissance Spain and the Hispanic heritage of its Santa Clara location. Maginnis was awarded the Gold Medal of Excellence in 1925 by the American Institute of Architects for his design. That same year the plans for the monastery chapel won first prize at the Paris International Exposition. It is considered to be the most perfect example of Spanish Renaissance Ecclesiastical architecture in the new world.

GROWING UP

Town growth and overcrowded conditions prompted the construction of a separate Santa Clara High School in 1905. The Santa Clara Grammar School, which had been built in 1867, housed both grammar and high school students until then. Over the next 30 years, enrollment increased three times and by 1900 had skyrocketed from less than 300 to 940 students. As a result, a bond issue election approved the construction of the high school on a block of land between Market and Bellomy, Main and Washington Streets. The school opened with 175 students and 10 faculty. In 1922, this building became the first intermediate school (sixth to eighth grades) in Santa Clara.

A FAMILIAR FACADE

By 1920 it had become clear that a larger high school building was needed. Expanding its original site by purchasing homes adjoining the existing high school, a second Santa Clara High School was opened in 1922. In addition to the new classroom building, shops and a gymnasium were also constructed. Santa Clara High remained the only high school in Santa Clara until 1959 when Buchser High School opened.

THE
MISSION
CITY
LOOK

One grammar school had filled the Town's needs for over 40 years and by 1912 it was clear to the school trustees that the building needed to be replaced. On the same site, the new Fremont School was constructed of reinforced concrete in an eye-catching mission-period style. Although the building was new, it was not wired for electricity and interior lighting came from skylights. It was not until the late 1940s that the school would be electrified. Fremont School served as the only elementary school until Washington School was built in 1932. These two schools met the needs of the Santa Clara community until the 1950s, an indication of the slow growth of the town over the preceding 100 years. Fremont School closed permanently in 1966 because of its failure to meet earthquake safety standards.

Margaret Jenkins, Bea Lichtenstein Collection

BLOOMER GIRLS

*The 1922 Santa Clara High School girls soft-
ball team is pictured in formal pose. Like the
typical American high school, Santa Clara
High provided competitive athletic opportunities for its students. Boys from the last quarter
of the 19th century participated in baseball,
football, track and later basketball. The options
were more limited for girls but softball, basketball and badminton were popular choices.*

Lemorad McKay's Clyde Arbuckle Collection

MUSIC MEN

*An early example of organized
cultural activity, the Mandolin
Club poses on the steps of Dr.
Paul's home.*

Clyde Arbuckle Collection

CULTURE [EN MASSE]

*Members of the Santa Clara Book Club hold a meeting and photo session at the Bray home on Scott's Lane. Formed
by members of the Shakespeare Club in 1895, by the beginning of the century it had 108 members with a library of
300 volumes. It would donate its collection to the Santa Clara Public Library when it opened in 1903. If the photo is
any indication, apparently no self-respecting matron would be found reading without wearing a proper hat.*

Santa Clara Historic Archives

MUSIC IN THE PARK

As the Plaza Park became more developed through the beautification efforts of the Woman's Club, a bandstand area was added in its center. It became a focal point for Sunday and holiday concerts as well as an easily identifiable meeting place. The bandstand was replaced by the Mission Branch Library in 1955. A replica of the bandstand is located today at the San Jose Historical Museum at Kelly Park in San Jose.

" ... THRESHOLD OF A NEW ERA "

The generation of Santa Clarans that spanned the Great Depression of the 1930s and the Cold War 1950s lived during a major transformation in their city. Sheer numbers indicate the magnitude of that change. In the 30 years preceding the outbreak of World War II, the city's population grew by about 33% to 6,650 residents. Within ten years it had grown another 75% and by 1960 almost nine-fold to 58,880.[1] No such growth of population could occur without creating dramatic economic, social and political changes. The president of Santa Clara University, Reverend William C. Gianera, S.J., in 1947 described the area as "on the threshold of a new era."[2]

But the 1930s anticipated few of those changes. The years of the Great Depression seemed to solidify Santa Clara's small town, agricultural orientation. While the depression decade saw widespread national unemployment, the orchardists of the area were always able to keep home-grown food on the table. The labor intensive nature of the fruit industry insured that the need for pickers and cannery workers remained relatively constant though seasonal. The proximity of the railroad to the city did bring an influx of transients during those hard times who daily formed a bread line at the rear of the University kitchen.[3] On the other hand, the City's residents were somewhat distracted from the harsh economic times and given a sense of local pride through the national publicity that surrounded the Alaska explorations and lectures of the Santa Clara priest, Bernard Hubbard, S.J., and the successes of the University's football teams, culminating in consecutive Sugar Bowl victories in 1937 and 1938, both over favored teams from Louisiana State University.

By the end of World War II, it is estimated that the Santa Clara Valley provided half the world with its processed, dried and fresh fruit and by 1960 it remained the world's largest center for these industries.[4] But changing economic times would end the dominance of agriculture. The Pratt-Low Preserving Company continued to can fruits and vegetables until 1960 when, after 55 years in Santa Clara, it leased its plant and sold its processing equipment to the Duffy-Mott Company. Duffy-Mott closed its operations in the mid-1970s. The Gangi

Brothers Packing Company came into its own immediately after the war, producing 150,000 cases of tomato paste in 1946, and some 600,000 cases annually by the early 1950s. But those glory years were short-lived and Gangi Brothers would ultimately move into the Central Valley. Mayfair Packing purchased the Rosenberg plant in Santa Clara in 1958 and added some new structures on its 15 acre site. Bucking the industry trend, Mayfair expanded its operations into the 1970s but ultimately gave way to the changing times.

Today, the last surviving packing company in Santa Clara is the Diana Fruit Company. Founded in 1921 on Monroe Street by Alexander Diana, an immigrant from Yugoslavia, it specialized in sweet cherries for fruit cocktails and maraschino cherries. Diana had developed a formula for preparing cherries that would not "bleed" and stain the other fruits in the mix. An employee and later son-in-law, Eugene Acronico, improved upon that formula and, when Diana died in 1941, he took over running the company. Diana Fruit would subsequently be sold and re-sold to national corporations and then bought back by a small group of investors. Eugene Acronico, Jr. currently serves as its president.

A number of the established manufacturing enterprises in Santa Clara similarly saw their businesses decline and replaced by new products and technologies.

BEFORE THE STORM
A serene overview of Santa Clara in 1940 on the verge of World War II. The university campus in the center faces cottages across the Alameda. Franklin Street, the heart of the business district, runs past the campus on the right and stops at Lincoln and the Carmelite Monastery. In the upper left, Homestead Road plunges into orchards after a few short blocks. Of particular note at the upper part of the photo is how close to "town" are the orchards and fields — a condition many current Santa Clarans can still remember.

BLESS 'EM ALL

The formal picture of the first annual Santa Clara City employees picnic captured virtually all of the City's employees and some County dignitaries at Uvas Dam in 1934. In one place were councilmen and meter readers, the water plant engineer and "the" City janitor, the City Attorney and men from the street department. The municipal infrastructure was a modest one.

Santa Clara Historic Archives

WHAT A DIFFERENCE THE YEARS MAKE

By the mid-1950s, the City's utilities department alone had almost half of the total number of City employees at the 1934 outing. The post-war City was growing, the demands for its services were increasing, and the number of City employees was rising.

The Eberhard Tannery, with its roots in the Mission period, suffered from a decline in the demand for leather as automobiles replaced horses (and their harnesses) and rubber replaced leather soles on shoes. A fire in 1933 destroyed half of its buildings and, after limping on for another 20 years, it closed and was sold to the University as a site for its new engineering complex. The Pacific Manufacturing Company ultimately experienced a similar fate. Although it operated double shifts as the war clouds built up in the late 1930s and expanded its operations during the war, the detailed millwork it did had become too costly to continue its profitability. When it failed to obtain an acceptable contract with its union employees, the Board of Directors decided in 1959 to dissolve the corporation and sell off its physical assets. Initially purchased by James Viso and Associates, its

warehouses were leased out for a number of years until Viso sold the property to the University for future expansion.

Representative of the industrial shift in Santa Clara from basic 19th century products like leather and wood to 20th century synthetic and composite manufacturing was the establishment of the Owens-Corning Fiberglass Corporation plant in 1948. Owens-Corning manufactured products from glass fibers into insulating materials and yarns. The corporation came west after the war and moved into a newly constructed plant that served as headquarters for the company's western division.

Located in a newly zoned industrial tract near Lafayette Street, this plant served notice that future industrial development would occur away from the Southern Pacific depot and "downtown" Santa Clara and onto former orchard land to the north and east of the City. It was a forerunner of the industrial and commercial development that subsequently spread across Highway 101 and brought about a series of annexation wars in the 1950s among competing municipalities. What had been a city of three square miles at its founding would soon encompass 20 square miles. Santa Clara was growing up and out.

As new businesses moved in, population grew and farm acreage declined. It was estimated that each new industrial job in the county brought with it eight to ten new residents while providing another one-and-a-half new non-manufacturing jobs. It was also claimed that every 100 new factory jobs meant four new retail stores opened.[5] Santa Clara, county and city, were in the midst of an unprecedented population boom and the demand for housing skyrocketed. Farmers sold to developers, orchards yielded to homes, and housing tracts sprang up in the western part of the City around Pruneridge Avenue with the bucolic but non- agricultural labels of Forest Park, Laurel Park, Westwood Oaks and San Tomas Woods.

The new population expected the services and environment they were accustomed to. Thus in 1949, the volunteer fire companies gave way to a paid fire department of six men and three new stations were built in the 1950s. The police department expanded to 23 men in 1951, augmented by the newly established Police Reserve of about 40 men. The quaint designation of City Marshal was changed in 1950 to Chief of Police. Six new

City parks were opened in the 1950s to complement the 17 new schools built in that decade. A bond issue that included funding for a new library building was passed in 1959 after similar issues had been defeated twice in the early 1950s. The Wutzit Club, later the Santa Clara Youth Village, began in the downtown area to address the problems of juvenile delinquency in the early 1940s. The Jefferson Youth Center opened its doors in 1959 to provide a gathering place for youth groups in the northern part of the City. And civic culture was augmented by the Santa Clara County Symphonette founded in 1950, soon renamed the Santa Clara Philharmonic. By 1960, residents of Santa Clara could look with pride at a city on the move.

The new population also expected more of its city government. The Board of Trustees only met monthly and the requirements of the growing city outpaced the administrative structure of the 1927 charter. Thus, in 1951, a new charter was approved by the voters that established a city manager form of government. The Board of Trustees became the City Council, which had the responsibility to hire a full-time professional city administrator whose job it was to organize and administer the various city government departments. Santa Clara had moved from basically part-time volunteer governance to full-time professional management. But decisions remained in the hands of the Council. One of the most far-reaching in its implications for the City was the Council's decision in 1958 to apply for federal funds from the Urban Renewal Administration. The Council, acting as the redevelopment agency, designated the old downtown area for demolition and rebuilding. Opposed by many of the downtown merchants, the razing of the eight square blocks ultimately took place and "downtown" Santa Clara disappeared. The growth and development of the City in the years to follow did not include the re-emergence of a new downtown.

GRIDIRON HEROES

Coach Lawrence T. (Buck) Shaw poses with some of his 1937 and 1938 Sugar Bowl champion Santa Clara Bronco football squad. Success on the football field brought welcome publicity to the school and to the town. On their first trip to New Orleans for the January 1, 1937 game, 200,000 individually wrapped prunes were distributed from the rear of the train during its stops and in the stadium. The labels heralded "Two Famous Santa Clara Valley Products: the Santa Clara Broncos and Santa Clara Prunes." Nationally, the name 'Santa Clara' became an even more familiar name.

NAME RECOGNITION

While the Pratt-Low label remained and its Santa Clara origin was highlighted, after 1960, the Pratt-Low Preserving Company was sold and became a division of the Duffy-Mott Company. After a decade and a half, Duffy-Mott discontinued its Santa Clara operations.

CHANGING TIMES

After operating for 43 years in Santa Clara, Rosenberg Bros. sold their facilities to the Mayfair Packing Company in 1958. Going against the trend that saw processing and drying plants relocating out of Santa Clara, Mayfair's owners, the Perrucci and Di Napoli families, expanded its walnut processing capacity to meet the demands of its world-wide export market. Although continuing to be a profitable enterprise, its urban setting and rising property values made its sale almost inevitable. In 1995 Mayfair sold its Santa Clara property to a developer who constructed a retail and office park on the site adjacent to the Southern Pacific depot.

THE SURVIVOR

While the picture shows the original Monroe Street location of the Diana Fruit Preserving Company, the company today is located on Mathew Street in the commercial and industrial area adjacent to de la Cruz Boulevard. Still specializing in various kinds of cherries, the fruit no longer comes from the Santa Clara Valley. Under its shortened name, The Diana Fruit Company is the sole survivor of the fruit industry that once helped to define Santa Clara.

V FOR VICTORY

Named for the Mission and City of Santa Clara, Mission Santa Clara, slides toward the water at its 1944 launching in Sausalito. As part of a crash ship-building program, this tanker took 64 days and nights to construct. Weighing 15,600 tons and 523 feet long, Mission Santa Clara *carried mostly gasoline to the fronts during the last year of the war.*

Santa Clara Historic Archives

James R. Bacigalupi Collection

PROUD PARENTS

Representatives of the University, the Chamber of Commerce and Mayor James Bacigalupi (second from left) celebrate the launching of the tanker Mission Santa Clara *on May 18, 1944.*

PREPAREDNESS

Santa Clara University Archives

As part of the war effort, an Army Specialized Training Program (ASTP) moved onto the University campus in May 1943. Designed to train men in basic and advanced engineering, it subsequently took over 75% of the campus. Although lasting only a year, it illustrated, together with a strong city enlistment rate, effective air raid warden system and the popularity of war bond sales, the wide-spread support of all segments of Santa Clara for the war.

VOLUNTEERS STILL

As it had for almost a century, Santa Clara continued to rely on volunteer fire fighters into the post-war years.

Although the separate companies merged into one volunteer force, each retained responsibility for a defined geographic

area and their own specific identity. Members of the Tanner Hose Company pose for this photograph in 1948.

PREPAREDNESS

In 1949, the City hired its first paid professional fire fighters, though the volunteers might argue that the only difference between them and the new team was the "paid" not the "professional" part. Five of the original six came from the volunteer hose companies. From left to right: Jess Rogers from Mission Hose, John Andrade from Hope Hose, Leonard George from Tanner Hose, Emil Flossi the exception from the San Jose Police Department, and Frank Toledo and George Koop from the Hope Hose Company. The men worked in 24 hour shifts, with one day off every 72 hours. When more paid fire fighters were added, Leonard George became the first paid Fire Chief.

OLD TIMER ON PARADE

Santa Clara's first motor-driven pump engine, an Ahrens Fox, purchased in 1927, is part of

this 1949 parade. Proudly driven by members of the new paid fire department, the Ahrens

Fox and a 1941 ladder and pumper truck were the only two engines on active duty. The

1913 Seagraves chemical truck served as standby in case of a dire emergency.

THE PRIDE OF SANTA CLARA

This horse-drawn steam pumper is readied for a late 1930s city parade. In the driver's seat is Tanner Hose company member and later Mayor James Bacigalupi. The owner of Dergan's Saloon on Franklin Street, Bacigalupi was mayor from 1942-1948.

READY FOR ACTION

The 'A' shift in 1949 mans all of its regular fire vehicles in front of the City's new firehouse on the corner of Benton and Main Streets. The fire house served as headquarters for both the paid and the volunteer fire fighters. Within a decade, three additional stations would open as the department expanded in size and equipment to serve the needs of the expanding City.

SIGNS OF PROGRESS

Motorcycle police became both more numerous and more necessary as more people acquired automobiles and traffic grew after World War II. When blue uniforms became the standard in 1948, the motorcycle officers retained their khakis for another nine years. Here are motorcycle officers Clarence Andrade and Manuel Sylvia flanked by Marshal O'Neill and Inspector Sapena.

A NEW ORDER

Edna Mirone became the first female member of the Santa Clara Police Department when she was hired as the first police matron in 1953. Her duties focused on internal operations. She assisted in female arrests, served as booking officer, operated the radio and teletype machine, handled the complaint desk, did the typing and kept the records. The first female patrol officer would be hired more than twenty years later in 1975.

PART OF THE THIN BLUE LINE

When the title of City Marshal was changed in 1950 to Chief of Police, the City Marshal, John O'Neill became the first to hold that designation. Aware that his force of 23 men was stretched thin for the growing city, O'Neill established the Santa Clara Auxiliary Police Force, now the Police Reserve. This group of about 40 men successfully augmented the regulars in their peacekeeping responsibilities.

THE BRIDGE BETWEEN PAST AND PRESENT

As the department expanded in the late 1940s, Frank Sapena was one of the new officers hired. He rose rapidly through the ranks to inspector and director of the Police Auxiliary. Santa Clara was one of the few cities where the chief of police was elected and, when Chief O'Neill retired, Sapena was elected Chief in 1955. He would supervise the growth of the department and its move to the new Civic Center headquarters. Sapena served as a bridge between the old Santa Clara and the new. He retired in 1975 after 20 years as Chief.

A FORMIDABLE FIGURE

The growing City anticipated the need to update its city governance practices. A new charter in 1951 created a council-manager form of government. The charter called for hiring a chief administrative officer to supervise the administrative functions of the City while the council attended to legislative matters. The first permanent City Manager, Joseph F. Base, was chosen by the council in late 1952. In his four years of service, he undertook to begin modernizing city services. His photo here looks anything but modern for the 1950s.

CRUSADE FOR FREEDOM

PILLARS OF THE LAW

EYES ON THE FUTURE

As the Cold War intensified in the early 1950s, programs to encourage patriotism, like the "Crusade for Freedom," became civic projects. As part of promoting one of these campaigns, City leaders are photographed. They include Judge Forrest Bentzien (left), Santa Clara's first Municipal Court Judge. As the City grew, its judicial structure was upgraded. Bentzien was first elected Justice of the Peace in 1934 and then to the sole judgeship in 1952. When he retired in 1969 he had served the people of Santa Clara for 35 years.

Judge Edwin J. Owens, for twenty years the Dean of Santa Clara University's law school, was appointed to the Superior Court in 1953. Here he administers the oath to his friend and former colleague at the law school, Joseph P. Kelly. Kelly became a Santa Clara Justice of the Peace in 1950 and in 1961 was appointed the city's second Municipal Court Judge. He would later become a superior court judge.

Founded by the energetic Reverend Walter Schmidt, S.J., of Santa Clara University, the Wutzit Club was formed during World War II to counteract a rising incidence of juvenile delinquency. The Club grew beyond anyone's wildest dreams and by 1947 had around 1,000 members. A great fundraiser, Fr. Schmidt brought Hollywood stars to headline benefits for the now renamed Santa Clara Youth Village. Its first benefit featuring Frank Sinatra raised $10,000 in 1947. Here Mayor James Bacigalupi is flanked by Buddy Baer and Sinatra.

PAUL J. DIAS

ATTORNEY AT LAW

of Am

S.C. DIS

A MORE MODERN
FESTA

Parades were an integral part of mid-20th
century Santa Clara. Here is the SES float
with the Holy Ghost queen and her
princesses in 1947 on Franklin Street in
downtown Santa Clara.

EVERYONE LOVES A PARADE

One of the many fraternal organizations that sponsored floats, the
Order of Redmen met for years in a suite of rooms above the Bank
of America at Franklin and Main Streets.

AND THE BEAT GOES ON

Formed in 1945 by the Santa Clara Young Man's Institute
(YMI), the Green Dragons contributed music and marching to
many City parades. As its reputation grew, it performed in
many different events and locations. It won marching bands
state championships for three consecutive years, 1947-49.

OLD ST. CLARE'S

Mission Santa Clara was the parish

church for Catholic families in Santa

Clara until it burned down in 1926.

When it was rebuilt, it became a chapel

for the University and a new parish

church was built across Lafayette Street

from the University. For a quarter century,

St. Clare's parish was the only Catholic

parish in the city.

COME TO THE STABLE

When St. Justin's parish was established in 1951 to serve Catholics on the west side of Santa Clara, its

temporary church was a remodeled stable on Gould Street (now Scott Boulevard). A permanent church,

hall and school were built later in the 1950s on five acres of prune orchard on Homestead Road. St.

Justin's men's club is still called "The Stablemates," recognizing the parish's humble beginnings.

BIRD'S-EYE VIEW

One of the first new industrial businesses to settle in the Santa Clara Valley after World War II, Owens-Corning

Fiberglass Corporation constructed a plant of nine buildings along Lafayette Street and what is now Central

Expressway. Reflecting the industrial growth of the City and the valley, the company' original 250 employees grew

by the 1970s to more than 1000. The picture captures both the openness of the land and the beginnings of growth.

BEGINNINGS

One of the early housing subdivisions, Killarney Farms, located

around Homestead Road' came from the land originally settled by

James M. Kenyon in the 1850s. He acquired move than 200 acres

and planted primarily hay and grain rather than fruit trees. Upon

his death in 1907, the land was divided among his children and

subsequently their children. Members of the Kenyon family are

present for the symbolic beginning of construction for Killarney

Farms.

" EVERYTHING'S CHANGED BUT THE TREE... "

The transformation of Santa Clara from an agricultural town to a metropolitan city that began in the 1950s continued through the rest of the 20th century. Many farming families sold their land for residential subdivisions, often moving into one of the new homes. The last orchard in the City was removed in 2000 for the construction of the new Kaiser Medical Center. Rapid post -World War II suburban growth was followed in the 1960s by the construction of many new public facilities to serve the community. In the 1970s, the focus shifted to industrial development as the City recognized the need for a balance between population and employment. The strength of Silicon Valley's electronics industry carried Santa Clara beyond such a balance into a position of great economic strength in the 1980s.

The changes prompted one wag to note " everything's changed but the tree."[1] The modern era started with one of the most controversial decisions the City has ever made—to demolish its original downtown in the hope of creating a new economic center for Santa Clara. The old downtown was a traditional small town center with both public facilities like City Hall and the jail, and commercial services including a market, five and dime and a movie theater. Using Federal Urban Renewal funds, eight blocks along Franklin Street were acquired and torn down. Those owners and businesses able to survive were relocated into the newly constructed two block Franklin Mall and the remaining six blocks were offered for new development. Nothing happened for many years and the last vacant parcel was not built upon until 1987. The Methodist Church across the street at Liberty (now Homestead Road) and Main Streets was rebuilt at Lincoln Street and Warburton Avenue. Liberty Tower, a high rise retirement residence, was built in its place.

c. 1950, Santa Clara Historic Archives

DOWNTOWN

This is a typical view of Franklin Street, which was the center of Santa Clara's small downtown. The horse drawn and later electrified trolleys ran from San Jose on The Alameda, turning west on Franklin.

Subdivisions of tract homes continued to expand in the 1960s. Santa Clara grew in size and established its current boundaries relative to the surrounding cities of San Jose, Sunnyvale and Cupertino. Natural and logical borders like the Guadalupe River, Calabazas Creek and Stevens Creek Boulevard were used in some cases, but in others the City limits were the result of the "annexation wars" that cities used to shape their community.

The earliest industrial development in Santa Clara was located along the Southern Pacific Railroad lines, first in the Old Quad area and later, in the 1950s and 60s, along Lafayette Street, north of the San Francisco rail line. Early industry was predominantly manufacturing and businesses supporting agriculture. Later the Owens Corning plant was built to supply insulation for the construction industry.

The beginning of the phenomenon known as Silicon Valley was associated with Stanford University and the development of the radio. In 1957, a group of eight scientists working for William Shockley and his laboratories left and founded Fairchild Semiconductor. There, the first integrated circuit was refined for commercial use. Within five years, the eight entrepreneurs

each left Fairchild to produce spin-off companies which became the seeds of Silicon Valley. The three of these companies of greatest influence on the city of Santa Clara were Intel Corporation, National Semiconductor and Advanced Micro Devices.

As many of the most well known companies of the growing computer industry moved into Santa Clara, a new type of development came with them: the industrial campus. Memorex Corporation built an award winning headquarters at San Tomas and Central Expressways. These new campuses and industrial parks were built with all the necessary streets and utilities, with landscaped frontages, parking lots and well-designed buildings. The City remains the headquarters location for Intel, National Semiconductor, Applied Materials and 3Com. Other major industrial employers include Agilent Technology, Nortel Networks, Sun Microsystems, Sanmina, Network Associates and Integrated Device Technology.

Intel was founded by Robert Noyce and Gordon Moore in 1968 and was soon joined by Andy Grove. Two of Intel's developments were critical to the growth of the computer industry— the microprocessor and large-scale integrated memory.[2] Near the beginning of 2002, Intel employed 7500 people in its Santa Clara facilities and 80,000 worldwide. At it's headquarters on Mission College Boulevard, Intel has built a museum to depict the history and development of the semiconductor industry.

Applied Materials is the world's largest producer of semiconductor manufacturing equipment.[3] From its 1967 origins in the Silicon Valley, it reached global markets with major facilities in Japan and the Far East. Today, Applied Materials employs 16,000 people worldwide.

Retail development also followed the population growth of the 1950s and 60s. El Camino Real became the prime commercial street in the City, eventually extending south from the San Francisco Peninsula to San Jose. Shopping centers like Mervyn's Plaza, Moonlite and Kmart were built at major intersections and a mixture of individual businesses and shops filled in between. Stevens Creek Boulevard, also a commercial strip along the southern edge of the City, has a different character. It is the auto row of the west valley, with virtually every carmaker represented.

Valley Fair was the area's first regional mall, originally constructed as two separate department stores, one in Santa Clara and one in San Jose. During two major expansions, it has grown into one uninterrupted, enclosed regional mall surrounded by parking structures, still straddling two city limits.

In response to this rapid growth, the community

TEMPORARY CO-EXISTENCE

This aerial shows the conversion of agricultural land to high technology. The early campuses were one and two stories high with excellent access to the freeways and expressways of the Valley. Corporate functions of administration, research and development and manufacturing were combined on one site.

undertook a tremendous public construction effort. Not only the City of Santa Clara but the Santa Clara Unified School District, the County of Santa Clara and the Santa Clara Valley Water District were all constructing facilities to support the changing Valley. In 1964, the City opened the new Civic Center, which combined City Hall, Police Administration and a County Court. The Triton Museum of Art was built on adjacent city-owned property. Later two historic homes, the Jamison-Brown House and Headen-Inman House were relocated to this property. Fire stations, arterial streets and utility expansions were completed to serve new development.

A major commitment to open space and recreation was made with the acquisition of Central Park, 52 acres in the middle of Santa Clara. Central Park became the home of the Central Library, the International Swim Center and the Community Recreation Center. Major

community events such as the Art and Wine Festival and the All City Fourth of July Picnic are held in the park. Throughout the growth of residential subdivisions, the City acquired neighborhood parks in every part of Santa Clara, preserving its open space and recreation opportunities. Three school districts serve the City with the Santa Clara Unified School District covering the majority. The Cupertino Union and Campbell Union Districts serve areas south of Pruneridge Avenue. At the peak public student enrollment, there were 19 elementary, three intermediate and three high schools in the City. Population shifts toward smaller and older families in the 1970s and 80s led to a 50 percent reduction in enrollment. Many schools were closed and some were sold for redevelopment. Today, there are 13 elementary schools, two intermediate and two high schools and five private elementary schools and two private high schools.

MISSION COLLEGE

The West Valley Mission Community College District obtained a 160 acre site at the interchange of Freeway 101 and Great America Parkway. The first phase of the college opened in 1976. Construction of subsequent phases was delayed due to changes in state funding levels. Surplus portions of the campus have been leased for a shopping center and office development, generating significant revenues for the district. This has allowed construction of a Library and Telecommunications Center, Child Development Center and Science and Technology Complex. Mission College has the equivalent of 10,000 full time students.

Paul Becker Photo, 2002, City of Santa Clara Collection

Santa Clara is within the West Valley/Mission Community College District with Mission College located north of the Bayshore Freeway and west of Great America Parkway.

The College's focus is to provide basic college education for working students and specialized training for high tech and hospitality jobs.

Along with the population growth of the 1950s and 60s, the City, as a governing institution, expanded to meet the needs of its citizens. New departments and divisions were added to provide increased services for the community. The seven member City Council, with a rotating Mayor, provided the policy and appointed the City Manager to serve as chief executive officer and administrator. The Council also appointed the City Attorney. The City Clerk and Police Chief were directly elected. The only significant change in this organization was the shift in 1969 to a directly elected Mayor for a term of four years. This gave the Mayor additional stature as political leader of the City and chair of the Council meetings. Former Mayors, not directly elected, were elected by the Council and served one year terms.

Gary G. Gillmor, the first elected Mayor, served from 1969 to 1977. Under his guidance, the City became known as the "Youth Sports Capital of the World." William Gissler, Mayor from 1977 through 1985, was a strong supporter of the City's electrical generation projects. Everett N. "Eddie" Souza served eight years from 1985 to 1994, opening the Convention Center and bringing the National Football League San Francisco 49ers headquarters and training facility to the City. The current Mayor is Judy Nadler, first elected in 1994 after serving eight years as a Council member, and reelected for a second term as Mayor in 1998. She led the transformation of the electric utility into Silicon Valley Power and stressed the need for open government.

In the City Clerk's office, which is responsible for all the City's records and election administration, Steve Belick was practically an institution of his own. He was the elected City Clerk from 1952 to 1983. Judy Boccignone has ably replaced Steve and continues to serve as City Clerk. As well as elections officer for the City, Judy has added the functions of City Auditor to the position.

The City Manager is the chief executive officer of Santa Clara. Donald "Don" Von Raesfeld replaced City Manager Lloyd Brady, in 1962. His was an extremely influential career with the city of Santa Clara, serving from 1962 to 1987 and finishing with a term as City Council member from 1988 to 1991. A special chapter of this book is devoted to city accomplishments under Don Von Raesfeld.

Santa Clara is unique in having a directly elected Police Chief. There have been several attempts to change to an appointed Chief but each was rejected by the voters. Steve Lodge, the current Chief, was elected in 2000. Charles Arolla served from 1994 to 2000. Frank Vasquez served from 1988 to 1994 and Manny Ferguson served for 12 years from 1975 through 1988. Frank Sapena, elected in 1955, served through 1975. All of these Chiefs were elected from the ranks of the City's Police force.

In the Fire Department, Leonard George served as Chief until 1975. The main Fire station was named after Leonard in honor of his many years of leadership. Don Visconti served as Chief from 1975 to 1986, followed by Robert Sharps from 1986 to 1993 and Gerald Simon to 1999. Phil Kleinheinz is Santa Clara's current Fire Chief

The 1980s ended with Santa Clara poised for the dramatic economic development of Silicon Valley. The population and educated workforce were in place. The basic street network and utilities were built, and public facilities were ready to serve the community.

SMALL TOWN HALL

In service from 1913 to 1963, this City Hall at Franklin and Washington Streets housed all municipal services except for the jail. It was replaced by the far larger Civic Center and was demolished with redevelopment of the downtown.

RURAL STILL

The Rumbolz farm complex on Homestead Road just west of San Tomas Expressway was a classic Santa Clara Valley compound of residential and agricultural structures. The surrounding orchard of plums kept the prune dehydrator supplied. It was eventually redeveloped with new single family homes on a private street and restoration of the main house. The water tank house was relocated to the city owned Harris-Lass Historic Preserve.

c.1960, Santa Clara Historic Collection Archives

c.1964, Santa Clara Historic Collection Archives

A FAMILY AFFAIR

Originally the site of the Santa Clara Coffee Club in 1903, the Red and White Central Market opened in 1919. It became Toledo's Market in 1928 and both Anthony Toledo and his market were institutions in old Santa Clara. Tony served on the City Council from 1943 to 1959 and was Mayor in his last year.

UNIVERSITY ELECTRIC

This unique false front building was originally a feed and grain store. University Electric moved to the corner of Franklin and Jackson after being displaced by urban renewal. The business relocated again to a larger store in the industrial area on Martin Avenue.

THE SILVER SCREEN

The theatre opened around 1920 and was operated in the 1920s and 30s by John Vasconcellos (grandfather of Santa Clara's long term state legislator). It met the silver screen needs of Santa Clara for many years until the construction of a large movie theatre on El Camino Real. An alternative movie experience was provided by the Moonlite Drive-in Theatre. Located behind the Moonlite Shopping Center, it was eventually replaced by condominiums. Next to the theatre was the Genova Delicatessen, operated by Joseph and Annita Bruna. Joe became owner in 1933 and ran the Deli until 1966.

1964, Santa Clara Historic Archives

A SANTA CLARA "JEWEL"

The origins of Wilson's Jewel Bakery date to 1891, when it operated as Universal Bakery. After a succession of owners, William A. Wilson bought the Jewel Bakery from Ignatz Felix in 1921. The Bakery grew until displaced by urban renewal. Wilson's Jewel Bakery was among the thirteen original property and business owners who decided to move into the new Franklin Mall development.

PETERSON'S INSURANCE

Established by Antone (Pete) Peterson in 1929, the business and building were bought by Joseph DeLozier in 1958. Following displacement in 1963, Peterson's Insurance located in the new DeLozier Building in Franklin Mall. Joe's son David was a Council member from 1988 through 1996 and a Chamber of Commerce director.

ODD FELLOWS

Santa Clara Lodge No. 52 of the International Order of Odd Fellows was organized on January 18, 1856. Their lodge was built in 1868 over first story stores at the corner of Franklin and Washington Streets. Wade's Mission Pharmacy was a tenant when the building was demolished by urban renewal and later located in Franklin Mall. Notice the John F. Kennedy campaign office.

HERE'S TO YOU!

This 1866 building was originally a bakery and then the Franklin Street Saloon and Rooming House. Martin Dergan acquired the business in 1886, changing the name to Dergan's Corner, and operating it for 50 years. It was purchased in 1936 by James Bacigalupi and continued until demolition in 1964. The business reopened at the corner of Kiely Boulevard and Homestead Road as New Dergan's.

M. E. Church, Santa Clara, Cal.

Tucker Photo

A TRADITION CONTINUED

Located at the corner of Main and Liberty (now Homestead

Road) Streets, this church replaced an earlier Methodist Church

which partially collapsed in the 1906 San Francisco Earthquake.

This church was itself rebuilt in 1965 on Linclon Street across

from the Civic Center. It was replaced by Liberty Tower.

↑ Visitor Parking
→ Employee Parking
↑ Employment Office
↑ Purchasing

NEW DESIGN

Built in 1970, the Memorex facilities were Santa Clara's first example of the new style industrial campus. Memorex was founded in 1961 and became the one of the largest producers of precision recording tape. The company had both financial and legal difficulties in the 1970s and was acquired by Burroughs in 1981. The entire campus had been demolished and redeveloped by 2001.

NEW FACILITIES FOR
intel

SIMPSON STRATTA & ASSOCIATES

HOWARD J. WHITE, INC.

TOWARD SILICON VALLEY

Intel's new building is shown under construction at the corner of Central Expressway and Bowers Avenue. This was Intel's first campus in Santa Clara and is still is use, although remodeled several times over the years. Silicon wafer fabrication goes through major cycles every few years, necessitating changes to the manufacturing facilities. State of the art "clean rooms" are required to prevent contamination of the wafer chips by minute particles of dust.

Paul Becker Photo, 2002, City of Santa Clara Collection

EQUIPMENT FOR CHIPS

Applied Materials has several campuses in Santa Clara including this one at Central Expressway and Scott Boulevard. As the prime supplier of equipment needed to fabricate chips, Applied Materials has risen with the success of companies like Intel, National Semiconductor and AMD.

Paul Becker Photo, 2002, City of Santa Clara Collection

TREES GROW WITH INDUSTRY

Twenty five years after construction, the early industrial parks of Santa Clara have become well landscaped environments. Companies in the buildings, or at least their names, change with surprising frequency, reflecting the volatile market of high technology.

MOONLITE BECOMES US

Like the industrial parks, the shopping centers of Santa Clara have evolved over the last several decades. Anchor tenants have changed, storefronts have been remodeled and landscaping has been planted in the parking lots. New tenants like video stores, nail shops, ethnic restaurants and coffee shops have moved in. The one constant at this center has been the bowling alley, Moonlite Lanes.

Paul Becker Photo, 2002, City of Santa Clara Collection

VALLEY TRANSPORTATION

Stevens Creek Boulevard is the boundary between Santa Clara and San Jose. But the two sides make up the original "auto row" in Santa Clara Valley. The large parking lots of new cars, the numerous signs and gleaming showrooms are the hallmarks of this street. Although all types of cars are sold here, the wealth of Silicon Valley supports many high end automobile dealers.

CIVIC CULTURE

The relocation and transformation of the City Hall into a Civic Center symbolized the changes Santa Clara was experiencing at the time. Construction began in 1962 and was completed in 1964. A small park and pool with a statue of Sainte Claire, at the top right of the photo, faces El Camino Real.

WILCOX VS. SANTA CLARA

Wilcox High School was built to serve new population in the north-western area of the city. As enrollment declined in the 1980s, Wilcox become one of two high schools to remain. The other, originally called Buchser, was renamed Santa Clara High to retain that historic name.

TRITON
MUSEUM OF ART

First located in temporary pavilions across from the Civic Center, the Triton Museum of Art held a design competition for its permanent building. The Triton has a number of holdings including the Austen Warburton Native American Collection and paintings by Theodore Wares.

c.1960, City of Santa Clara Collection

*Lloyd E. Brady was the second City
Manager under the new City Charter,
appointed in March 1957. A major capital improvements bond issue was passed
under his leadership enabling the city to
modernize many public facilities.*

A STRONG HAND

*Donald R. Von Raesfeld became the City
Manager in 1962 and served for nearly 25
years. He guided the City through a period of
rapid growth of employment from 25,000 to
more than 100,000 jobs. He was involved in
many of the major decisions shaping Santa
Clara as a modern city.*

City of Santa Clara Collection

City of Santa Clara Collection

FRANK SAPENA
SERVICE: 1955-1975

City of Santa Clara Collection

DONALD FERGUSON
SERVICE: 1975-1988

City of Santa Clara Collection

FRANK VASQUEZ
SERVICE: 1988-1994

City of Santa Clara Collection

CHARLES AROLLA
SERVICE: 1994-2000

City of Santa Clara Collection

STEVEN LODGE
SERVICE: 2000-

EVER EXPANDING

The early Mission Library in the Old Quad area of Santa Clara was soon overwhelmed by the influx of new residents. A new library was opened in 1967 in Central Park with 36,000 square feet. It was designed by Edward Durrell Stone, a noted modern architect, with concrete arches and skylights. The Central Library was one of the most used city facilities and was expanded in 1980 to 44,000 square feet. It was demolished in 2001 to make way for the new Central Park Library.

FAMILY FUN

One of the major events of the Santa Clara season is the Art and Wine Festival. Held in Central Park, it brings together residents and visitors for artwork, crafts, wine and beer tasting. Local non-profit groups sell food and beverages for fund raising. Profits from space rentals and tasting are donated to community charities.

MAKING AN INTERNATIONAL SPLASH

The Swim Center in Central Park was dedicated on September 10, 1967 as one of the finest outdoor aquatic facilities in the world. It uses solar panels to heat the pools. The Center has hosted international swimming, diving and synchronized swimming competitions, as well as pre-Olympic events. More than 20 world swimming records have been set at the pool.

DONALD R. VON RAESFELD

In a position notorious in many other cities for turnover, Don's length of service as City Manager was outstanding. He administered the City with a firm hand, combining fiscal conservation and an entrepreneurial spirit.

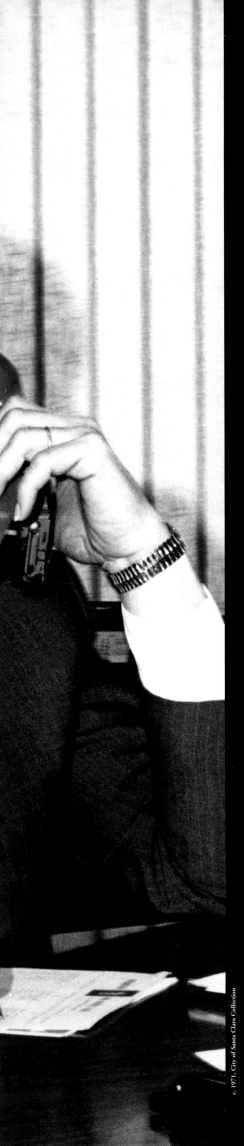

DONALD VON RAESFELD

"...RUN WITH A PRIVATE SECTOR, RETURN-ON-INVESTMENT MENTALITY"

Since 1960, no single person has had more influence on the shape of Santa Clara than Donald R. Von Raesfeld. His commitment was less to a career than to a city.

Don was born in 1927 in San Jose. His father was an accountant with Standard Oil and commuted by train to San Francisco. Don attended Bellarmine High School and Santa Clara University, graduating with a degree in Civil Engineering. His first job was with the California Water Service in San Jose.

The City of Santa Clara hired Don in 1957 to work as its Water Superintendent and shortly after promoted him to the Director of Public Works and Utilities. His continuing interests in financing public infrastructure and municipal utilities were established in these years. In February 1962, out of a field of more than 150 applicants, the City Council unanimously appointed Don as City Manager. In his first annual report to the Council and community, Don listed among the accomplishments: initiation of the new Civic Center and Corporation Yard, ongoing construction of the Sewage Treatment Plant, major street improvements and conversion of utility billing to electronic data processing.[1]

The specific accomplishments of Don Von Raesfeld ("Don Von" or "DVR" to his employees) during his career as City Manager were numerous. He directed the building boom of public facilities in the 1960s, necessary to keep pace with the growing population. His two major achievements were the creation of the Bayshore North Redevelopment Area in 1972 and the development of the city-owned electrical generation projects.

The Bayshore Redevelopment Area was the financial catalyst for development of the northwest section of the City. The Redevelopment Area has funded major public infrastructure and facilities like the Convention Center, Golf Course, purchase of the Theme Park and planned parking structure, as well as affordable housing throughout the City.

The City's electric utility became a nationally recognized municipal utility under Don's leadership. Through participation with other municipalities, Santa Clara was able to lever its size and benefit from the construction of several large power generation projects.

Equally important was Don's style of leadership that grew to permeate the organization and still influences the staff today through his successor, Jennifer Sparacino, and the many department heads who served under him and didn't retire until the 1990s. Befitting his engineering background, Don was a hands on, detail oriented manager who still saw the big picture. These abilities served him well in Council meetings and budget discussions with department heads. His extreme frugality was legendary among City staff.

He was an interesting mix of conservative with taxpayers' money and very innovative in terms of governmental enterprises. A book entitled "Reinventing Government" used two of Don's successes as examples of "How the entrepreneurial spirit is transforming the public sector."[2] The book discusses the City purchase of the

Great America Theme Park as an unusual municipal action that was financially beneficial, preserved a valued community facility and avoided the traffic impacts that redevelopment of the park could have created. The second example in the book is the innovative electric and solar utilities in Santa Clara.

May 19,1972, was declared *"Don Von Raesfeld Day"* in a celebration coordinated by the Santa Clara Chamber of Commerce and the Citizens Advisory Committee. After 25 years of service, he retired in 1987. Not content to rest on his laurels, Don ran for City Council and served one term from 1988 through 1992. He was also active in the Santa Clara Chamber of Commerce, serving on its Board of Directors and as Chair.

Don's dedication to public service is not only reflected in his career. Among his nine children, one is the Fire Marshal for the City, two others have been fire fighters in other jurisdictions, one is a public school teacher, one works for the Valley Transportation Authority and another for the County Sherif's Department. His public spirit has clearly been passed on to the next generation of his family.

"HT2– HIGH TECH, HUMAN TOUCH."

The research and development sectors of high technology drove a dramatic construction and real estate boom in the decade of the 1980s. As computers became an essential part of the global economy and individual life Santa Clara's businesses reaped the benefits. The national recession around 1990 brought this initial boom to an end. Many new commercial structures sat as empty "see through" buildings for several years. The mid 1990s saw a communications industry boom with a tremendous burst of new Internet businesses. Aggressive entrepreneurs and their employees made fortunes in stock values. That bubble burst in 2001 and the new century was off to a slow economic start for Santa Clara and Silicon Valley.

The focus of much of the Santa Clara's development in recent years has been within the Bayshore North Redevelopment Area. Originally created in 1972, the Redevelopment Area became the financial vehicle to provide public utilities and services for the area as well as the locations of two special projects; Marriott's Great America Theme Park (now owned by Paramount Parks) and the Marriott Hotel.

A FAIRYLAND

The double decker Carousel Columbia is located in the entrance plaza of Paramount's Great America Theme Park. It is 100 feet tall and features 103 carefully detailed figures. Each figure is a replica of a famous original.

These became the catalysts for considerable new development and the start of Santa Clara's visitor economy. The City's Convention Center, Westin Hotel (originally a Doubletree Hotel), Techmart offices and Golf and Tennis Club were all built around 1985 through the actions of the Redevelopment Agency. Although privately financed, the hotel and offices are built on city-owned land and pay significant lease revenues to the City.

The Agency was also the means by which the City was able to preserve the Great America Theme Park when the Marriott Corporation wanted to sell it for development. Through a decision later ratified by the voters, the City's purchase of the Theme Park retained thousands of jobs for youths and supported the City's visitor-oriented economy. The Bayshore North Redevelopment Area also generates millions of dollars a year that are spent on affordable housing for the community.

Santa Clara University's history has paralleled the City's in many ways, from its initial founding in 1851 to its ride on the wave of the Silicon Valley's economic prosperity. In the last two decades, under the leadership of its presidents William Rewak, S.J. and Paul Locatelli, S.J., the University has become a highly respected national educational institution. Its graduate schools of Law and Business have groomed many leaders of the Valley, both past and present. The University celebrated its Sesquicentennial in 2001 and published a commemorative book entitled, "Serving the Intellect, Touching the Heart."[1]

The relocation of El Camino Real from the center of the campus to its eastern edge enabled the University to consolidate its layout. This cooperative project among the University, City of Santa Clara and the State of California opened a new front door for the campus and added vacant land for expansion. Successful fund raising campaigns have enabled Santa Clara University to build new facilities for the library, law school, communications, science, recreation and residences. Adding to the University's recent fame was its women's soccer team, which won the national title for the first time in 2001.

Santa Clara has had a long history as a source of athletes and during the 1960s was known as the "Youth Sports Capital of the World." In 1928, Margaret Jenkins, a resident, was the first woman from Santa Clara to participate in track and field at the Olympics. In the Olympics during the decade of the 1960s, thirteen Santa Clara residents or athletes training here won medals. The Santa Clara Swim Club, coached by George Haines, became a model for the development of championship swimmers. Pablo Morales, Donna de Varona, Mark Spitz, Steve Clark, Dick Roth and Claudia Kolb Thomas, among others, all trained and competed at the City's swim center. The center was renamed in 2000 the George F. Haines International Swim Center. More recently, the Santa Clara synchronized swimming team, the Santa Clara Aquamaids, achieved championship status, both in club competitions and the Summer Olympics.

In professional sports the San Francisco 49ers NFL football team maintains its headquarters and training facility in Santa Clara on land leased from the City.

In 1987 Jennifer Sparacino succeeded Don Von Raesfeld as City Manager. She was previously a deputy in the Manager's office and before that in the Department of Parks and Recreation. She has led the City through many major accomplishments, including the restructuring of the City's electric utility as Silicon Valley Power to successfully compete in the deregulated power environment. She is now overseeing the redevelopment of a large surplus state hospital to a Sun Microsystems campus and a complete new neighborhood with 3,000 dwellings. Working with a succession of Councils, she has maintained the City's enviable financial condition, allowing the new construction of several major public facilities.

As many of the public facilities of the 1960s have aged and been outgrown, Santa Clara has initiated a new round of construction. The new Police Administration building was opened in 2000, located on the rerouted El Camino Real near the historic railroad depot. Central Library has been demolished and a new Central Park Library, nearly twice as large, will replace it by 2004. A new fire training facility and station on Walsh Avenue is under way. In the Parks and Recreation Department, the Youth Activity Center, Teen Center and Skateboard Park have been built on the Cabrillo Intermediate School grounds. Planning for the expansion of the Senior Center is in progress.

While looking to the future, Santa Clara has not neglected its past. During this period, the City purchased and restored two major historical landmarks. The Harris-

Lass house, circa 1865, and related buildings are a fine example of an orchard farm typical of this Valley. Older and more significant is the Berryessa Adobe built in the late 1840s. It is the only example of a residential adobe and the oldest house left in Santa Clara. Equally notable are the families associated with the Adobe, as representatives of the pre-American Californio culture and the later immigrants from Europe.

Although not a public facility, the non-profit Kaiser Medical Center has provided important medical coverage for many Santa Clara residents. Built in the 1960s to serve the growing population, its buildings are also showing their age. In 2001, Kaiser began construction of a replacement Medical Center at the corner of Lawrence Expressway and Homestead Road, which will be far larger and will offer the most modern medical services to its members.

Since its founding in 1888, the Agnews State Hospital has played an important role in the city of Santa Clara. Originally opened as a mental asylum, the hospital was the focus of a small village housing employees and a station on the South Pacific Coast Railroad. The hospital was devastated by the 1906 Earthquake and more than a hundred inmates and staff lost their lives.[2]

1999, City of Santa Clara Collection

AN EYE TOWARD YOUTH

In response to the resurgence of interest in skateboarding, the City's Youth Commission recommended to the City Council construction of a skate park. The new park was opened in September 1999 on the grounds of Cabrillo Intermediate School, adjacent to the Youth Activity Center. It is designed for both skateboarders and in-line skaters with 15,000 square feet of skating area featuring rails, curbs and bowls.

Paul Becker Photo, 2002. City of Santa Clara Collection

TIME MARCHES ON

The centerpiece of the post 1906 Agnews Hospital, the Clock Tower was completely renovated by Sun Microsystems to be the focal point and visitor center for their new campus.

Dr. Leonard Stocking undertook the reconstruction of the hospital, basing the design on the approach of treating the mentally ill rather than simply restraining them. The physical layout was a campus style, combining the dormitories and service facilities into a practically self-sustaining complex. In the 1960s, the state began to phase out many of its facilities for the mentally ill in favor of more community based ones. Agnews was converted to a Developmental Center caring for those with severe mental or physical disabilities. By the 1990s the patient population had declined to such a point that Agnews in Santa Clara was declared surplus by the State of California and offered for sale.

By 1997, the 320 acre Agnews campus was the largest property in the City with redevelopment potential. The decision of what to do with its open space, historic buildings, trees and wildlife became a very important community issue. After a lengthy process of proposals, negotiations, hearings, an election and a lawsuit, Sun Microsystems built a campus for 3,000 employees while rehabilitating four historic structures and providing a 14 acre open space easement for the community. On the rest of the site, a new neighborhood called Rivermark with housing, shopping, school, a branch library, fire station, police substation and parks, has begun construction. Affordable housing for seniors, families, developmentally disabled and the homeless are all a part of this new neighborhood.

In the later decades of the 20th century the character of the City's population growth began to change. The early post war expansion was fueled primarily by emigration from the rest of the country. In 1960, Caucasians made up the vast majority of the population.[3] By 1980, however, immigration from Latin America and Asia was well underway. The Caucasian population at that time was 73% with Hispanics at 15% and Asians at 9%. Vietnamese and Filipino were important components of this Asian growth.[4] By the year 2000, new immigrants from Korea and India were adding to the mix of Santa Clara's population. Now the Caucasian population was 55%, Hispanics 16% and Asians had increased to 29%.[5]

This growing diversity of the community is reflected in the types and ownership of local businesses, particularly along El Camino Real. Here new residents are participating in America's entrepreneurial opportunities and serving the needs of their fellow immigrants. Although not as obvious, these new citizens are involved in the Valley's high tech businesses as well, both as technical employees and as entrepreneurs.

Another important change in Santa Clara is the growth in the older segments of the population. In 1958, residents over 65 years old made up 6% of the City.[6] By 2000, this percentage had increased to nearly 11%.[7] The median age was 33 in 2000. Individuals living alone made up one quarter of all the households in Santa Clara. At the same time, the school age population had declined dramatically and the demand for City services was changing to reflect the community's composition.

Because Santa Clara has had its own electric utility since 1896, the City was particularly affected by California's deregulation of the power industry. Beginning in the 1980s, the City has invested in renewable and independent sources of power to provide the cheapest, most reliable electricity for its residents and businesses. As part of a campaign to protect itself from the financial storms of deregulation, the City's utility became Silicon Valley Power. A long term strategic plan was adopted by the City Council with the resulting successful transition to a more market-driven utility. Silicon Valley Power is now the third largest municipally owned utility in the state.

Just prior to its Sesquicentennial year, the City of Santa Clara achieved another distinction. In 2001, the National Civic League named Santa Clara as one of only ten All-America Cities in the nation. After submitting its application, the City was selected as a finalist and invited to Atlanta, Georgia, to participate in the June awards competition. Santa Clara's delegation consisted of elected and city officials, organization representatives and community members from a variety of backgrounds. The City's presentation stressed the history of Santa Clara and its responses to the challenges of affordable housing, youth recreation and the reuse of Agnews Hospital. The team used the theme and logo *HT2 - High Tech, Human Touch*,[8] symbolizing the accomplishments of the commu-

nity while retaining ties with its residents. The announcement of the City's 2001 win has been the source of great celebration and civic pride.

The year 2002 represents the culmination of three Sesquicentennial years: the City of Santa Clara in 2002, the Santa Clara University in 2001 and the State of California in 2000. The City participated in all of these celebrations. The year 2000 was marked by the construction of Sesquicentennial Park at the corner of El Camino Real and Lincoln Street. Markers there discuss the role of the "Battle of Santa Clara" in the events leading to statehood. The City and the University have jointly published a compilation of lectures on "Telling the Santa Clara Story, Sesquicentennial Voices," edited by Russell K. Skowronek.

The City's Sesquicentennial year has been marked by a series of events starting on March 9 with the dedication of an El Camino Real bell at the Woman's Club Adobe. On May 18, the Berryessa Adobe was dedicated as a restored historic landmark. Each of the families who had lived in the Adobe since the 1840's were in attendance. Special musical and theatrical performances were held throughout the year.

The actual Sesquicentennial date was celebrated on July 4, 2002 with an All-City Picnic and fireworks display at Central Park. Dignitaries from local and state governments, as well as our sister city Izumo, Japan, were in attendance. A ceremony involving all the flags flown over the City and the reading of a special poem by Suzanne Cisneros highlighted the day.

In the fall, special dedications of the historic Santa Clara Railroad Tower and the new Veteran's Memorial in Central Park were held.

The year concluded with the dedication of the "Stroll into the Past" display of history markers at the Civic Center and the publication of this Sesquicentennial commemorative book.

GREAT AMERICA

This aerial of the Theme Park was taken in

1976, the year the park opened to coincide

with the nation's bicentennial celebration. The

Marriott Corporation originally built and

operated the park in concert with a similar

park in Illinois. When Marriott decided to sell

the park in 1985, the city stepped in to pur-

chase and preserve Great America. The park

business was later sold to Paramount Parks,

but Santa Clara retains ownership of the land.

GETTING TOGETHER

A visitor-oriented complex of a Convention Center, Westin Hotel, Techmart offices, Golf and Tennis Club and conference/ banquet facilities have been built on city-owned land at the corner of Great America Parkway and Tasman Drive. This view shows, from the left, the Techmart, Westin and Convention Center with the Golf Course in the rear.

A PLACE TO STAY

The Westin Hotel was opened in 1986 and has 500 rooms. It is directly connected to the Convention Center and shares the large ballroom and kitchen in the Center.

WELCOME TO SANTA CLARA

The Convention Center was financed by the City Redevelopment Agency and opened in 1986. It is successfully operated by the Santa Clara Chamber of Commerce/Convention and Visitors Bureau.

FORE!

The new municipal Golf and Tennis Club opened in 1987. Helping to dedicate the sports facility were, from left to right, Mayor Eddie Souza and City Council members Sue Lasher, Judy Nadler, Vern Deto, John Mahan and Jim Ash.

A PLACE TO PLAY

The course is within an easy walk of the Convention Center and Westin Hotel. It replaced a smaller municipal course that has been redeveloped for housing and a 40 acre Ulistac Natural Preserve along the Guadalupe River. Most of the new course is built on a closed landfill, creating a variety of terrains in an otherwise level City.

HIGH STYLE

A recent addition to the Bayshore North Redevelopment Area, this building was constructed by Sobrato Development and is occupied by Verifone.

GRIDIRON GLORY

When the San Francisco 49ers football team was looking to replace its aging facility on the Peninsula, Santa Clara proposed ten acres of city-owned land. A ground lease was negotiated and the 49ers constructed their new headquarters in 1988. With two grass and one artificial turf fields, they can prepare for all upcoming game situations.

A NEW HOME FOR A MODERN FORCE

The Police building in the 1964 Civic Center was added to and remodeled to accommodate the growing department. When the city realized that the Civic Center was too small for a new building, a site at the corner of El Camino Real and Benton Street was chosen for the new police headquarters. It was opened in October 2000 and is designed with room for the department to expand.

JENNIFER SPARACINO

Jennifer Sparacino was appointed City Manager on March 8, 1987 and continues to lead the city administration through the Sesquicentennial year.

WINNERS

In 1995, three new members were inducted into the Santa Clara Swim Center Hall of Fame. Left to right, Pablo Morales, winner of three gold and two silver medals in the 1984 and 1992 Olympics; Earl Carmichael, in the center, retired Director of Parks and Recreation and George Haines, former head coach of the Santa Clara Swim Club. Under Haines' direction, the Swim Club won 43 medals in three Olympics.

AT HOME IN THE WATER

The Santa Clara Aquamaids, founded in 1964, train at the Santa Clara Swim Center. At the 1996 Summer Olympics at Atlanta, the U.S. Synchronized Swimming Team, which included four members of the Santa Clara Aquamaids, won the gold medal. From left to right in the photo are Larry Wolfe, Director of Parks and Recreation, Becky Dyroen-Lancer, Chris Carver, head coach of the Aquamaids since 1984 and Olympics coach, Suzannah Bianco, Jill Sudduth and Heather Simmons-Carrasco.

MUSIC MAKERS

The Santa Clara Vanguard Drum & Bugle Corps was formed in 1967 as a non-profit youth organization. The championship Vanguard was the first corps in the Drum Corps International to have two corps in the top 25 at the same time.

A GROWING CAMPUS

The Communication, Public Policy and Applied Ethics Building was part the Santa Clara University

1997 Five-Year Master Plan. It was the major academic facility built in that expansion effort.

UNIVERSITY UNITED

After the relocation of El Camino Real to the east side of the university, The Alameda, which bisected the campus, was closed to traffic. It was replaced with a landscaped mall creating an attractive north-south axis for the university. During construction of the mall, railroad ties from the trolley line that once connected Santa Clara and San Jose were unearthed.

A DIVERSE COMMUNITY

The business community of the City is also changing. Many signs on El Camino Real are now in Korean and Vietnamese. Shops cater to Mexican, Indian, Pakistani and Middle Eastern residents.

A CIVIC PARTNERSHIP

Completely renovated by Sun, the historic Agnews auditorium serves both as a meeting and training facility for Sun and as a cultural space for the public. Under a unique agreement, the auditorium can be reserved by the city for public use on certain evenings and weekends.

OLD AND NEW

Sun constructed new two and three story buildings around the historic core of the old Agnews Hospital. A 14 acre easement encompassing the four historic buildings and many heritage trees was granted to the City, allowing public access to the campus during the day. The new buildings are designed to highlight the historic structures. When fully built out, the new campus will accommodate more than 3000 employees.

2001, Group 4 / Architecture, City of Santa Clara Collection

BOOKS AND MORE

This is a sketch of the new library entrance which will face Homestead Road. The new facility will be nearly twice as large as the old one and will feature underground parking, state of the art technology and will open out to Central Park on the north. It will be completed in 2004.

TO YOUR HEALTH

2000, Anshen + Allen, Architects

This perspective of the replacement Kaiser Center is a bird's eye view from over Homestead Road. The medical center will include greatly enlarged medical offices and outpatient treatment facilities, a new hospital and parking structure. The site will be extensively landscaped and borders the Calabazas Creek.

PAGE 164   "HT2-HIGH TECH, HUMAN TOUCH."

2000, City of Santa Clara Collection

HOMETOWN ADVANTAGE

As part of its adjustment to the deregulated power environment, the City's Silicon Valley Power initiated an advertising campaign to educate customers of the benefits of municipally owned electricity. When the energy crisis hit the state in 2000, the same campaign was shifted to encourage conservation.

ALL AMERICAN CITY

This shield is the symbol of the city's recognition as an All America City in 2001, one of only ten in the country.

2001, National Civic League

" ...IT'S GOING TO BE AN EXCITING WORLD ..."

The differences between Santa Clara at incorporation in 1852 and now are obvious: the size of the community, the environment of the Santa Clara Valley, the political and social world around us, and, of course, the technology. The similarities are less obvious. Local government with locally elected representatives hasn't changed too much. Our population is still a mixture of native-born and recent residents. Santa Clara is still a magnet for immigration with new cultures and languages adding to the diversity of the community.

How will the look of Santa Clara change in the next 25 years? Because the City is largely built out and policies are in place to retain the single-family subdivisions, the overall character of the community will not change significantly. The dramatic growth of housing in the 50s and 60s and the industrial booms of the 80s and 90s will probably not be repeated in the near future. Redevelopment will occur in older industrial and commercial areas. The resulting construction will be a higher density than that it replaces. Buildings will be somewhat taller and there will be a tendency to mix uses more. For instance, along El Camino Real, residences will be built above or behind stores and offices.

In single family neighborhoods, houses will continue to be remodeled to fit the needs of the residents. Larger homes are necessary for extended families, new rooms will allow different activities to occur without conflict, and second stories will be added because of the rising cost of land. Since most trees in the City were planted since 1950, they will grow to become larger and more prominent in Santa Clara.

The economy of the City and Silicon Valley will certainly change. Already, the dominance of the computer hardware companies is shifting. The software and telecommunications sectors have become a larger portion of the local high tech industry, although the recent Internet bust dampened that growth. In the longer run, there are other high tech sectors that will be attracted to the quality labor, venture capital and educational institutions in this area. Joint Venture: Silicon Valley Network has identified three such industries; information technology, biotechnology and nanotechnology (the science of molecular manufacturing[1]).[2] Advances in these fields will have dramatic impacts on the environment of our economy. This in turn will gradually change the physical environment of the Valley.

Transportation has always been an important factor in the patterns of settlement. Wagons and stagecoaches, railroads, cars and planes have all shaped the Santa Clara that we know. The proposed extensions of the Bay Area Rapid Transit (BART) line from Fremont and the Valley Transportation Authority's light rail lines will certainly improve transportation capacity in the Valley but are unlikely to substantially reduce the commute congestion on freeways and expressways. Fundamental changes in the way we work or the technology of transportation will probably be needed to achieve that goal.

There are no signs that the growing changes in Santa Clara's population will end. The aging of the current residents and immigration from around the world will soon result in a community with no majority and no minorities. Ethnic cuisines, religions of the world, languages and races are all becoming integral parts of the City. The globalization of economy and cultures will blur the divisions among our residents and between the United States and the rest of the world.

Certainly there will be hurdles in the City's future-the economic cycles, traffic congestion and high housing costs-but the strengths of the Santa Clara over the last 150 years have proven equal to previous challenges. Santa Clara's Sesquicentennial theme has been *"150 years of democracy, diversity and distinction."* The conjunction of a beautiful location, constantly renewing population and a spirit of innovation will carry the City of Santa Clara into the coming years. As David Packard once said, we have "wonderful futures to look forward to... it's going to be an exciting world."[3]

FOREWORD

1. Erin M. Reilly, "A River ran Through It." *Research Manuscript on the Cultural and Natural History of Santa Clara, No. 3.* Santa Clara University, 1994; Grant William Schick, "The Ohlone and the Oak Woodlands: Cultural Adaptation in the Santa Clara Valley." *Research Manuscript on the Cultural and Natural History of Santa Clara, No. 4.* Santa Clara University, 1994; Joanna M. Blume, "Grasslands—The Forgotten Resource: The Cultural Ecology of the Central California Grasslands." *Research Manuscript Series on the Cultural and Natural History of Santa Clara, No. 1.* Santa Clara University, 1994.
2. Ethnographic information, courtesy Mark Hylkema, M.A., 2002)
3. In one of the earliest descriptions of the Ohlone, written in 1771, Don Pedro Fages describes them as follows: "It is first to be noted that those of the Valle de San Francisco [The Santa Clara Valley] are the ones who have the most culture and are the least savage. They have their hemispherical houses of about four yard's diameter, and they live very sociably, fixing their residences in large villages which…they abandon [in the spring] for the purpose of passing this…season in little brush houses which they construct at a short distance from their villages…They are provided with many and various seeds for their sustenance; and they do not lack for any kind of birds and land animals and timber." Pedro Fages, *A Historical and Political and Natural History of California by Pedro Fages, Soldier of Spain: Written for the Viceroy in 1775.* Translated by H. I. Priestly. (1937, reprinted 1972), 69.
4. Randall Milliken, *A Time of Little Choice: The Disintegration of Tribal Culture in the San Francisco Bay Area 1769-1810.* (1995), 66.
5. Malcom Margolin, *The Ohlone Way: Indian Life in the San Francisco-Monterey Bay Area*, 30.
6. Peter Browning, ed., *The Discovery of San Francisco Bay: The Portola Expedition of 1769-1779: The Diary of Miguel Costansó.* (1992), 119.
7. This term, literally "people of reason," was used to mean "civilized" (i.e., Spanish-speaking, Christianized).
8. While camped at San Francisquito Creek with the 1769 Portola expedition, Father Juan Crespi wrote this description in his diary: "…a plain some six leagues long, grown with good oaks and live oaks, and with much other timber in the neighborhood. This plain has two good arroyos with a good flow of water, and at the southern end of the estuary there is a good river, with plenty of water, which passes through the plain mentioned, well wooded on its banks (Guadalupe River)…This entire port is surrounded by many and large villages of barbarous heathens who are very affable, mild, and docile, and very generous. Stephen M. Payne, *Santa Clara County: Harvest of Change.* (1987), 18.
9. Herbert E. Bolton, *Anza's California Expeditions. III, The San Francisco Colony.* (1930), 143.
10. Mark G. Hylkema, "Archaeological investigations at the Third Location of Mission Santa Clara de Asís: The Murguía Mission, 1781-1818" (CA-SCL-30/H). Manuscript on file, Oakland. CA: California Department of Transportation, District 4 (1995), 19.
11. *Ibid*, 21.
12. Arthur D. Spearman, S. J., *The Five Franciscan Churches of Mission Santa Clara 1777-1825.* (1963), 25.
13. Hylkema, "Archaeological Investigations", 22.
14. Dorothy Krell, ed., *A Sunset Book: The California Missions: A Pictorial History.* (1981), 168.
15. Shown on map entitled "Spanish Roads to the Redwoods." Alan Brown, *Sawpits in the Spanish Redwoods 1787-1849.* (1966).
16. Marguerite E. Wilbur, ed., Vancouver in California 1792-1794: The Original Accounts of George Vancouver. (1954),.43. Note: The Peña Adobe (the Santa Clara Woman's Club) is one of the neophyte houses described by Vancouver and the only extant structure from the third mission site. These structures were also commented on by Alexander Forbes in 1839. In his book on California he wrote, "In the mission of Santa Clara, which in several respects excels the others, the houses of the Indians form five rows or streets which compared with the old straw huts must be considered really comfortable and this is the greatest improvement that has taken place in the domestic civilization of these people at the missions." Alexander Forbes, California: A History of Upper and Lower California. (Originally published 1839, London, reprinted, San Francisco, 1937), 3.
17. Mark G. Hylkema, "Archaeological Investigations."
18. Russell K. Skowronek, "Rediscovering the 4th Mission Santa Clara Church." Paper presented at the California Mission Studies Association Annual Meeting. (February 17 1996), 1.
19. Mayordomo was the title given to the secular overseer in charge of managing the mission land and all work at the mission.
20. In 1883, Nasario Galindo wrote a manuscript of his father's recollections of life at Mission Santa Clara. Included was the following about the construction of the last complex: "Having built all the houses in the square for the use of the priests, he [Juan Ygnacio Alviso] then built similar houses for the soldiers of the guard. As soon as these houses were finished he moved the priests to the new mission, as well as the soldiers and the officer in charge of the guard. He then commenced the houses for the nuns and the young single neophytes, after which he commenced the building of the church…When the church was finished it was whitened with plaster, which the Indians brought from the Sierra, and then it was painted." "Early Days at Mission Santa Clara: Recollections of Nasario Galindo," *California Historical Society Quarterly* (June 1959), 107-108. The original 1883 manuscript is in the possession of Mrs. Christina Alviso Chapman who also translated the manuscript.
21. Secularization means transferring from ecclesiastical (church) use to civil or lay use. Under the 1834 Act of Secularization, the confiscation of the California mission establishments began, with the government ordering the missions and all their lands turned over to the state. From 1834 to 1836, over eight million acres of mission land was opened to private ownership.
22. In 1834 there were 1,400 neophyte Indians belonging to Mission Santa Clara, by 1839 the number had been reduced to 300. Only five were able to obtain land grants from the Mexican government. Yñigo was granted 'Rancho Posolmi' located in Mountain View, Marcelo Pío and Cristóbal received 'Rancho Ulistác' near Alviso, and

José Ramón and José Gorgonio were granted 'Rancho La Purísima Concepción' in Los Altos Hills. Frank Soulé, John H. Gihon, M. D., and James Nisbet, *The Annals of San Francisco and History of California.* (1854), 61; Phyllis Filiberti Butler, Old Santa Clara Valley: A Guide to Historic Buildings from Palo Alto to Gilroy. (rev. ed.1991), 70; Clyde Arbuckle and Ralph Rambo, *Santa Clara County Ranchos.* (2nd ed. 1973).
23. Hubert H. Bancroft, *The History of California.* Volume III, 1825-1840. (1886), 728.
24. Forty-one grants were made in Santa Clara County, mostly from fertile mission lands.
25. By 1835, San Jose numbered approximately 700 people, 40 of these foreigners. Payne, Santa Clara County, 39.
26. Russell K. Skowronek and Lorie Garcia, "The Economic Legacy of Mission Santa Clara de Asís in the early American Period." Paper presented at the California Mission Studies Association Annual Meeting (February 18 1995), 7.

CHAPTER ONE

1. By 1836 he served as the Hudson Bay Company's agent in Alta California and held a few positions in the San José government. In 1841 Forbes moved to Monterey, where he became the British vice-consul. He was grantee of 'Rancho El Potrero de Santa Clara' in 1844, and in 1846 he was involved with Father Real in the initial development of what would become the New Almaden quicksilver mine. In 1847 he played a role in the Battle of Santa Clara. Dorothy F. Regnery, *The Battle of Santa Clara*, 124. Later he built and operated the "Santa Rosa Brand" flour mill in Los Gatos. Lorie Garcia, "Santa Clara: From Mission to Municipality." Research Manuscript Series on the Cultural and Natural History of Santa Clara, No. 8. (Santa Clara University, 1997), 16.
2. Edwin Bryant, *What I saw in California.* (Lincoln, Nebraska: University of Nebraska Press, 1985. Originally published by D. Appleton, New York, 1848) p. 318.
3. Mabel D. Early, "*A Biographical Narrative of the Bennett Family Pioneers of '43.*" (Unpublished manuscript in possession of Paul Conrado, Ukiah, California, n.d), 8; Edwin Bryant, *What I saw in California.* (1848, reprinted 1985), 318.
4. He later married Mary Bennett's daughter Catherine. He was 45 and she 21. The marriage was subsequently annulled. Early manuscript, 9-13.
5. The first emigrant party to take American wagons and American cattle over the summit of the Sierras into California was the Murphy-Stephens party. It arrived in November 1844, opening the California Trail.
6. California was placed on a war footing with all male citizens including naturalized citizens ordered into the army. Lorie Garcia, "Our Special Place." Paper presented at the American Planning Association National Conference, (1994), 12.
7. And, as wartime conditions existed between Mexico and the United States, almost all the men in the immigrant parties were immediately enlisted in the newly formed *California Battalion*.
8. The Charles M. Imus party reached the western slope of the Sierras the first week of October, arriving at Mission Santa Clara on October 15. Next, a portion of the Dickenson-Gordon party arrived. They had reached Sutter's Fort on October 16, 1846. The small party with Thomas and William Campbell and their families arrived in the Santa Clara Valley about the 25th of October. The last wagon train of the "Great Migration" to safely cross the Sierras (the Donner Party was behind them), arrived at Sutter's Fort on October 25th, and there the Harlan-Young party rested after their arduous 6-month trek, exhausted, with several members ill from typhoid. On November 9th they left for Santa Clara, where they had been informed by Fremont and the newspaper *California* they could spend the winter, reaching the mission on November 22, 1846.
9. Dorothy Wilson Fine. "A Fine Branch of the family Tree." (MS in possession of author, San Jose, CA, 1991), 39. One immigrant gave the following description of conditions in Santa Clara in a letter home in December 1846: "We found things in great confusion and times very hard. We are in Santa Clara, about 150 miles south of Sutter's fort, and a beautiful place it is. If you can picture yourself a solid mass of houses built of mud with scarcely a window or fireplace; fire in one corner and a hole in the roof for smoke to pass out; almost every one sick, without care; most of the men in the lower country with Fremont; surrounded by Californians, expecting every day to be attacked by them; beef and bread to eat; flour $8 a 100 pound and thankful for that; raining most of the time, you can form some idea how we live" (Isbell 1846).
10. Americans who had arrived earlier allied with the new immigrants, although since Bellomy had married María Bernal, a Californio, some immigrants questioned his loyalties and when "in December Father Suárez del Real sent Indians onto the steep roof of the granary to try to stop the leaks, the immigrants misinterpreted the effort as an attempt to force them to leave and halted the helpful endeavor by brandishing their guns." Regnery, 52.
11. The first school in Santa Clara was founded in the fall of 1846 by Olive Isbell in a stable in the mission compound with the purpose of keeping the immigrants' children from going outside the Mission walls, where it was felt danger awaited from the Mexicans who were at war with the United States. For the "schoolroom" an old stable was cleaned out with a hole cut in the roof to let out smoke and let in air. The books used were those brought in the immigrant wagons, and having no pen or inks available, Mrs. Isbell wrote her lessons with a pointed stick on the hard dirt floor. Gerald McKevitt, S. J., *The University of Santa Clara: A History 1851-1977*, 37.
12. This "battle" which took place on the open plain about two miles from the mission, was a result of several rancheros rebelling against Americans taking their livestock and property. (In his diary on February 5, 1847, Walter Colton wrote: "*Nor should it be forgotten that the Californians evinced … a disposition well suited to bring about an amicable treaty. They took up arms, not to make war on the American Flag, but in vindication of their rights as citizens of California, and in defense of their property.*" It was actually a two hour skirmish, not a battle; no one was killed, and the only casualty was the American military forces' cannon which continually bogged down in the knee-deep mud. A peaceful treaty was arranged on January 7, 1847.
13. Phyllis Filiberti Butler, *Old Santa Clara Valley: A Guide to Historic Buildings from Palo Alto to Gilroy.* (1975, reprinted 199), 70.
14. McKevitt, 32.
15. Although the sales were later declared null and void by Mason in 1848, the recorda-

tion of the first official survey of the Town of Santa Clara in 1866 shows the land was continuously occupied by settlers from 1847 on, as Henry Bee and Frank Lightston each attested: *"… that he knows the Town of Santa Clara …was established in good faith in the year 1847… and … this [1866] map correctly represents the blocks streets and squares of the said town as surveyed in the year 1847; and … says that the land embraced within the said survey of 1847 has been occupied and used for town purposes ever since."*

16. General Mariano Guadalupe Vallejo in his history of California writes: *"Gold in the mines! This cry, resounding throughout the length and breadth of California, created a veritable revolution, social and financial. The farmer left his plough in the furrow, the schoolmaster abandoned his books and blackboards, the sailor deserted his ship, the barber flung down his razor and the tailor his shears. Even the lover relinquished the hand of his sweetheart to clutch the pick and shovel and rush forth in search of the longed for metal."*

17. That he prospered is witnessed by the encounter with him described by the prominent southern Californian, Antonio Coronel, in August of 1848: "Upon arrival at the San Joaquin River in the Tulare Valley, we met Father José María Suárez del Real, who was a true vaquero and who had a great deal of gold with him. He told us that he came from Stanislaus Camp--recently discovered--which was a placer rich in gold. We went there and found … one or two Americans or foreigners, and several other parties of Spanish people who came from San Jose and other nearby points."

18. Only a few patches of the wheat crop had been harvested, so flour was mainly brought from Chile and the price climbed to $20 a barrel and onions brought $2 a pound. As labor of every kind became very costly, the price of limber climbed exceedingly high, with a charge of $100 per 1000 feet to haul it from Campbell's mill (near present-day Saratoga) to San Jose.

19. While immigrants entering the area prior to 1848 had caused problems by squatting on mission and rancho lands, these were minor compared to the impact caused by the onslaught of people entering the area following the discovery of gold. Five land grants had been made in 1844 and 1845 from land neighboring the mission compound, so when the first wave of immigrants arrived at Mission Santa Clara in 1846 this land was not readily available. Nonetheless, the land immediately adjacent to the mission buildings was, and parts were quickly settled by the new arrivals, and four of the grants quickly passed into American hands. 'Rancho Los Coches' had been granted to Roberto and 'Ulistác' to Marcelo Pío and Cristobál, all three Santa Clara Mission Indians. In 1847, Roberto sold 'Los Coches' to Antonio Suñol. When Marcelo Pío received 'Ulistác' in 1846, he was ninety-six years old, and soon after American occupation Jacob Hoppe gained possession of it for $60. The largest, 'El Potrero de Santa Clara,' was granted to James Alexander Forbes in 1844. He sold it to Commodore Robert F. Stockton in 1847. Finally, The 'Enright Tract' was granted in 1844 to Francisco García, and it passed into the possession of James Enright, an 1846 American immigrant.

20. This was in operation by 1849 as Chester Lyman's diary entry on Friday, April 14, 1849, noted that he "dined at Bellamy's [sic] at Santa Clara." Patricia Loomis, *Signposts II.* (1985), 21-22.

21. When in 1844, Lorenzo Pinedo constructed the first frame house in Santa Clara on his property at Santa Clara and Alviso Streets, it was considered a "great architectural event" in Santa Clara, as a frame house was a novelty.

22. Eugene T. Sawyer, *History of Santa Clara County* (1922), 277.

23. Cuttings taken from the mission pear orchard provided the start of some small early orchards. For example, in 1856, Thomas Fallon's pears won First Prize at the first State Agricultural Fair, held in San Jose. These came from his pear orchard in San Jose, which had been established by utilizing cuttings from the mission pear orchard. San Jose Telegraph (October 21, 1856).

24. Grain, particularly wheat, had been grown in the mission's fields, but it wasn't until the Americans arrived that the Santa Clara Valley's commercial farming period began, with wheat the dominant crop during the first three decades after Statehood. "The soil was so rich and the yields so high that the fields on Commodore Stockton's ranch, 'Rancho El Potrero de Santa Clara,' produced grain for ten years without any soil supplement." Lorie Garcia, "Santa Clara: From Mission to Municipality." *Research Manuscript Series on the Cultural and Natural History of Santa Clara, No. 8.* (Santa Clara University, 1997), 46.

25. Janice Marschner, *California 1850 A Snapshot in Time.* (2000), 1.

26. By the middle of 1849, the population had become so large and diverse that it was obvious that governing the people in California under the existing conditions of government and laws was impossible. Anticipating official Statehood, Governor Riley issued a proclamation in June for a Constitutional Convention to meet in Monterey on September 1, 1849. Within six weeks, the delegates to the Convention had "framed a state constitution that settled the slavery issue, established the boundary between California and Mexico, adopted the state seal and motto, and provided for state legislative and judicial officers." On November 13, 1849, an election in which only American citizens could vote, ratified the constitution and elected Peter Burnett as governor. San Jose was selected as the state capitol and there on December 20, 1849, General Riley resigned his gubernatorial office and Governor Burnett was sworn in. Although by a vote of her citizens California declared for statehood, ratified a constitution and elected a governor, there would be no official recognition until a Statehood Bill was approved by the United States Congress and signed by the President. The subject of California's admission to the Union was brought before Congress when President Zachary Taylor recommended the admission of California in his annual message at the beginning of January 1850. The debate in Congress continued from March through August, and on August 13, 1850 the Senate passed the California Bill on a vote of 34 to 18. Finally on September 7th, it passed in the House - ayes, 150; noes, 56; all the Southern congressmen voting against it. The bill then went to the President, and on September 9th Millard Fillmore who, by the death of Zachary Taylor, had succeeded to the presidency, signed it, and California was admitted as the thirty-first State.

27. The official 1850 U.S. Census was lost en route to the census Office; the 1849 county population of nearly 4,000 and the 6,764 counted in 1852 provide a basis for estimating the 1850 population.

28. McKevitt, 23.

29. *Ibid.*, 24.

30. *Ibid.*, 27.

31. Daniel D. Hruby, *Mines to Medicine: The Exciting years of Judge Myles O'Connor, His Hospital and the Pioneer physicians of the Santa Clara Valley.* (1965), 57.

32. Alice Hare, *Santa Clara Past and Present. Santa Clara News.* (March 15, 1910).

33. Ted Olin Harrison, A Determination of Eligibility for the Santa Clara Depot of the Southern Pacific Railroad Company. (Document on file with the California Department of Transportation, District 4. (1981), 5.

34. Charlene Detlefs, "Flour Milling in Santa Clara County 1840-1898." (Unpublished Master's thesis, Department of Social Science, San Jose State University, San Jose, CA, 1985).

35. Sawyer,. 277.

36. Austen Den Warburton, *Santa Clara Sagas.* Mary Jo Ignoffo, ed., Local History Studies Vol. 36, California History Center & Foundation (1996), 17.

37. A plaque located on the northeast corner of Winchester and Bellomy marks the site of the University of the Pacific.

38. "Old In Years Santa Clara Young In Goals." San Jose Mercury-News (January 30, 1972).

MARY BENNETT

1. Paul Conrado, Bennett Family descendant, (Personal communication with Lorie Garcia, June 2002.)

2. Mabel D. Early, "Biographical Narrative of Bennett Family." The Pony Express. Vol. XVII No. 4 No. 196 (September 1950), 8.

3. Edwin Bryant, *What I saw in California.* (1848, reprinted 1985), 318.

4. "The Black Knight of Zayante," *The Pony Express.* Vol. XX No. 6 No. 234 (November 1953), 6.

5. Frank F. Latta, Joaquin Murrieta and His Horse Gangs. (1980), 306. "His (Bennett's) wife, Mary, was a good woman but one of masculine attributes, who had a 'mind of her own' and a body also; in many respects head of the family."

6. "Mary Bennett, The Widow." *Riptide Centennial Edition* (Santa Cruz, CA) Vol. 22 No. 43 (October 1950).

7. The California Census of 1852: Counties of San Luis Obispo, Santa Barbara, Santa Clara, Santa Cruz, Shasta. Volume IX, 65.8 The White Caps, whose name was derived from their disguise, were a group of men who assumed the function of administrating punishment for what they perceived as offenses against the community. Their acts ranged from warnings to leave the neighborhood to violence and murder.

8. The White Caps, whose name was derived from their disguise, were a group of men who assumed the function of administrating punishment for what they perceived as offenses against the community. Their acts ranged from warnings to leave the neighborhood to violence and murder.

9. William Heath Davis, *Seventy-five Years in California.* (San Francisco, CA: John Howell-Books, 1967) p.149. Davis married into Californio society and lived in San Francisco from 1838 until he died. Active as a merchant, ship-owner, civic official and town founder, at one time he owned much San Francisco property. Mary shopped in his store located on the northwest corner of Clay and Montgomery Streets.

10. In November 1836 Juan Bautista Alvarado found support from Graham, leader of the American Mountain men, for his aim to overthrow Mexican rule. This force, comprised of the best riflemen in California enabled Alvarado to force the surrender of the Mexican Governor Nicholás Gutiérrez, and free Alta California from Mexican rule for the next few years, until in 1839, Alvarado himself was appointed governor by the Mexican government. In 1840 Alvarado, once again loyal to Mexico, was informed that Isaac Graham and his American followers planned to overthrow this government. This information led to Graham and a few of his followers being placed under arrest on April 7th, followed by the Californios arrest of 120 foreigners throughout the rest of the month, all of whom were sent to Mexico to stand trial. Lorie Garcia, "An American, a Governor, and a Priest: Decision and Denouncement." Paper presented at the California Mission Studies Association 16th Annual Conference (February, 1999).

11. Edwin Bryant described Mary as a "widow…who, with her family of sons, has taken up her residence in one of the buildings of the mission, and in the land grant confirmation hearings, James Alexander Forbes testified that in 1846 she lived in a small adobe house near the mission road to Alviso; a road which followed a route very close to that taken by the El Camino re-route of today.

12. Dorothy F. Regnery, *The Battle of Santa Clara.* (1978), 96.

13. "Mary Bennett, The Widow." Riptide Centennial Edition (October 1950).

14. *Ibid.*

15. *The Pacific* (Santa Cruz, CA) *Sentinel* (May 9, 1859).

16. Garcia, "Santa Clara: From Mission to Municipality," (revised edition, 2001), 42-44, 96, 100.

17. *Ibid.*, 96,100.

18. Latta, Murrieta, 306.

19. No. 237 "Coroners Inquest of Harry Love, June 29, 1868. Filed August 10, 1868." (State of California, County of Santa Clara.)

20. An article in the *San Jose Mercury Herald*, June 4, 1950, "Historic House" identifies her house as located at 1385 Grant St.

21. Early "Manuscript," 14.

22. Regnery, 93.

23. *Ibid.*

24. "Captain Joseph Aram," *The (San Jose, CA) Pioneer*, (April & May 1899).

25. Latta, 306.

CHAPTER TWO

1. Town Records of Santa Clara.

2. Annie Hitt, "S.C. Changes 100-Year-Old City Form." San Jose Mercury-News, (December 31, 1951).

3. Advertisement for the Stockton Rancho Nursery Stock, *The California Farmer*, (December 1854).

4. On March 3, 1851, Congress passed a law for the settlement of private land claims in California, establishing a three-member land commission located in San Francisco to settle the disputes between those who claimed Mexican title and those who squatted on the land. Frederic Hall, *The History of San Jose and Surroundings.* (1871), 334.

5. Bayard Taylor, *New Pictures from California*. (Oakland, CA: Biobooks, 1951) p. 17. Commenting on the striking difference made by the growth which occurred between 1849 and 1859, Bayard Taylor wrote: "A further drive…brought us to Santa Clara. The old…Mission with its long adobe walls, tiled roof, quaint…church, and orchards hedged with the fruit bearing cactus, were the same as ever; but beyond them, on all sides extended a checkerwork of new streets—brick stores, churches, smiling cottages, in the midst of gardens and orchards…The old avenue of trees still connects Santa Clara with San José; but as we drove along it, I looked in vain for the open plain covered with its growth of wild mustard."
6. Lt. Chris Baldwin, S.C.P.D., "The Peacekeepers." (Unpublished document, n.d.).
7. *Ibid.*
8. *Ibid.*
9. Stephen Payne, *Santa Clara County: Harvest of Change*, 68.
10. William A. Wulf, Los Gatos Historian.
11. Patricia Loomis, Signposts II (1985), 53.
12. Payne, 155.
13. John Cook to Santa Clara County. October-November Bill (1853.)
14. Lorie Garcia, "Our Special Place." Paper presented at the American Planning Association National Conference (1994), 27.
15. Ted Olin Harrison. "A Determination of Eligibility for the Santa Clara Depot of the Southern Pacific Railroad Company." California Department of Transportation, District 4. (1981), 5.
16. Santa Clara Depot informational flyer. (Santa Clara, CA: South Bay Historical Railroad Society, 1964.)
17. Harrison. "A Determination of Eligibility," 2.
18. *Ibid*, 3.
19. *Ibid*, 6.
20. Sr. Marie of St. Joseph, SND, translator, "Annals of the Santa Clara House." College of Notre Dame Archives, Belmont CA, (n.d.).

CHAPTER THREE

1. William Rucker, had immigrated with his family to California in 1852, from Virginia via Missouri, as a part of Benjamin Campbell's party and built a small Southern Methodist chapel next to their home in Santa Clara. His daughter, Margaret, born after their arrival in California, was 12 years old when Abraham Lincoln was assassinated. The day word was received of his death the household was disturbed by men coming up to their house and William went out to see what they wanted. The men insisted that the Chapel's altar be draped in the black crepe which they had brought, as mourning for the President's death. William refused to"adorn" his altar in black as a gesture of grief, which he did not feel, because "that would mock God." The men became angry, demanding that the altar be so draped, or they would burn the Chapel and house. Faced with leaving his family homeless, William took the black crepe and gave it to 12 year old Margaret. He had her drape the altar because the young girl knew nothing of politics, and thus it would not "mock God." Satisfied, the men left. Margaret had saved the family's home and Chapel, but was left in the terror of that day. Consequently, for the rest of her life,the family never uttered Lincoln's name in her presence. (Charles Berry, Rucker descendant).
2. *The Daily Alta California*, October 8, 1865.
3. "Poll Lists of the Election Districts of the County of Santa Clara General Election." Santa Clara Election District, Santa Clara Precinct. (1868), 73-87.
4. When Abram Block founded the Block Fruit Company, he brought in Chinese laborers, housing them on his property. According to Santa Clara Fire Department records, "an attempt to burn down the area on August 9, 1877 destroyed several of the Chinese quarters before the fire was put out."
5. Ronald Campbell, "Andrew J. Roll: An Oral History Interview." Santa Clara City Library. (1998), 15.
6. *Ibid*, p.14.
7. Other qualities credited to Santa Clara by H. S. Foote in his 1888 book, *Pen Pictures from the Garden of the World* were "*It is handsomely laid out and beautifully ornamented with shrubbery, flowers and plants. It is a quiet place as becomes a seat of learning, and is much sought after as a place of residence…the social nature of its intelligent people render it especially desirable for this purpose,*" ending with "*It is the historic spot of this county.*" Foote, 205.
8. William F. Hayward, "Pacific Manufacturing Company." (Santa Clara: Unpublished document, n.d.).
9. J. P. Munro-Fraser, *History of Santa Clara County, California*. (1881), 550.
10. Hayward, "Pacific Manufacturing Company."
11. In 1856, William Lent had constructed a home on his 95 acre estate and in 1866 James Pieronnet Pierce purchased it, along with 79 acres, for $48,000, renaming the home New Park.
12. Amanda Miller, "History of Home of Santa Clara Carmelite Monastery," *Hero of Call of the Wild* was born on Bond Ranch. It was the home of J. P. Pierce, Originator of Pierce Grape. *San Jose Mercury Herald*, February 25, 1923.
13. Bruce A. Macgregor and Richard Truesdale, *A Centennial South Pacific Coast*. (1982), 116.
14. Patricia Loomis, "Bethlehem's Star No Longer Shining," *San Jose News*, December 20, 1974.
15. Macgregor and Truesdale, 124.
16. Mark A. Hylkema, "Archeological Survey Report for the Proposed Relocation of the City Police Station Project City of Santa Clara Santa Clara County, California." City of Santa Clara Community Services Department. (1996), 7-8.
17. "Town of Santa Clara Annual Report for the Year 1902-1903."

JOHN MONTGOMERY

1. In 1996, his 1883 glider was named an International Historic Mechanical Engineering Landmark.
2. Mark D. Ardema, Joseph Mack , and W. J. Adams, Jr., " John Joseph Montgomery 1883 Glider." Official Program. The American Society of Mechanical Engineers designated Montgomery's 1883 glider as an International Historic Mechanical Engineering Landmark, May 11, 1996.
3. De Witt Rucker, a young student at Santa Clara in 1905, later recalled the following: "The old timers will remember the first flight of Montgomery's aeroplane. It was an exciting occasion. A balloon was filled in the old vineyard next to Father Ricard's observatory. The older boys held the ropes under instructions from Father Bell. At last the signal to go was given, and the balloon shot into the air. Attached to it was the little Montgomery glider, with Professor Maloney, the aviator of the day, clad in red tights, hanging on to it for dear life. Higher and higher it went. At last Maloney cut loose and came gliding down, making many wonderful sweeps and glides as he landed. Some say he was up over 3500 feet. At any rate, I believe it was the first successful flight on record. What a thrill it was!" *The Monthly Santa Claran* Vol. 8 (1937).
4. No one who witnessed this tragedy ever forgot it. Sixty-nine years later, Andrew J. Roll, who had been present as a young boy, related the following: "He just veered toward the south… we all looked, were looking up and watching. Apparently everything was all right and then, one of the wings collapsed, and within a fraction of a second or two, the other wing collapsed, and then, he came plummeting to the ground and was killed." "Andrew J. Roll: An Oral History Interview" conducted by Ronald Campbell on July 22, 1974. Santa Clara City Library (1998), 29.
5. Arthur Dunning Spearman, S. J., John Joseph Montgomery 1858 - 1911 *Father of Basic Flying*. (1977),124.
6. At the same time that the Wright Brothers were making their low-powered flight over Kitty Hawk, Montgomery's sophisticated glider was soaring 4,000 feet over the Santa Clara valley, under control and landing at a predetermined site. However, it wasn't until the advent of the electronic industry and the resultant development of the computer industry that the west coast gained credibility and its innovations/inventions obtained precedence over those of the east coast, so recognition of Montgomery's achievement was ignored; a situation which remains to this day, although he has received some limited attention. In 1946, Hollywood made a film about his life, "Gallant Journey," starring Glenn Ford and Janet Blair, and today Montgomery's craft "The Evergreen," restored by the Smithsonian National Air and Space Museum, is on display at the San Diego Aerospace Museum, and a replica of the "Santa Clara," with Maloney at the controls, may be seen at the Hiller Aircraft Museum in San Carlos.

CHAPTER FOUR

1. Gerald McKevitt, S.J., *The University of Santa Clara: A History, 1851-1977*, 132-33.
2. *Progressive Santa Clara*, Santa Clara Commercial League (1904).
3. Yvonne Jacobson, *Passing Farms, Enduring Values: California's Santa Clara Valley*, x.
4. John Mack Faragher, et al. *One out of Many*. v. II (1994), 655.
5. Alexis de Tocqueville, Democracy in America. ed., Richard D. Hefner (1956), 95.
6. *Santa Clara News*, June 12, 1906.
7. Austen D. Warburton, *Santa Clara Sagas*, 20-21.

CHAPTER FIVE

1. *The City of Santa Clara Invites Industry* (1964), n.p.
2. *The Monthly Santa Claran* (January 1947), n.p.
3. *The Santa Clara*, December 10, 1931.
4. Yvonne Jacobson, *Passing Farms, Enduring Values*, x and 226. In 1960, the county had 85 canneries, 23 dried fruit plants, 25 frozen food operations and 85 fresh fruit and vegetable packers, plus numerous dehydrators.
5. Stephen M. Payne, *Santa Clara County: Harvest of Change*, 175.

CHAPTER SIX

1. Roger Wise, " Santa Clara Redevelopment Agency Closing It's Books, *The Mercury*, Aug 23, 1971, Title Quote
2. Ward Winslow, ed.,The Making of Silicon Valley: A One Hundred Year Renaissance (1995).
3. *Ibid.*

DON VON RAESFELD

1. Title quote taken from David Osborne and Ted Gaebler, *Reinventing Government* (1992).
2. City of Santa Clara, 1962 Annual Report (1963).
3. David Osborne and Ted Gaebler, *Reinventing Government* (1992).

CHAPTER SEVEN

1. George F. Giacomini Jr. and Gerald McKevitt, S.J., *Serving the Intellect, Touching the Heart: A Portrait of Santa Clara University*.
2. Phyllis Filiberti Butler, *The Valley of Santa Clara, Historic Buildings* , 1792-1920 (1975).
3. *1960 U.S. Census*.
4. *1980 U.S. Census*.
5. *2000 U.S. Census*.
6. *Report on a General Plan for the City of Santa Clara* (1959).
7. 2000 U.S. Census.
8. City's Slogan as part of the application for the "All America City 2001" competition.

THE FUTURE

1. *Nano Technology Magazine* website, www.nonozine.com, April 15,2002.
2. Joint Venture: Silicon Valley, *Next Silicon Valley: Riding the Waves of Innovation*, December 2001.
3. Ward Winslow, ed., Quoted from David Packard,*The Making of Silicon Valley: A One Hundred Year Renaissance* (1995).